China Geographer

China Geographer

Number 12: Environment

edited by Clifton W. Pannell
and Christopher L. Salter

LONDON AND NEW YORK

Dedicated to the memory of
JOSEPH E. SPENCER (1907–1984)

First publishing 1985 by Westview Press, Inc.

Published 2018 by Routledge
52 Vanderbilt Avenue, New York, NY 10017
2 Park Square, Milton Park, Abingdon, Oxon OX14 4RN

Routledge is an imprint of the Taylor & Francis Group, an informa business

Copyright © 1985 Taylor & Francis

All rights reserved. No part of this book may be reprinted or reproduced or utilised in any form or by any electronic, mechanical, or other means, now known or hereafter invented, including photocopying and recording, or in any information storage or retrieval system, without permission in writing from the publishers.

Notice:
Product or corporate names may be trademarks or registered trademarks, and are used only for identification and explanation without intent to infringe.

Library of Congress Catalog Card Number: 78-645067
ISSN: 0162-0789

ISBN 13: 978-0-367-01227-4 (hbk)
ISBN 13: 978-0-367-16214-6 (pbk)

CLIFTON W. PANNELL, Editor

Department of Geography, University of Georgia, Athens, GA 30602
Telephone: (404) 542-2856

CHRISTOPHER L. SALTER, Coeditor

Department of Geography, University of California, Los Angeles, CA 90024
Telephone: (213) 825-1071

EDITORIAL ADVISORY BOARD

Sen-dou Chang, University of Hawàii, Manoa
Norton Ginsburg, University of Chicago
Ronald Knapp, State University of New York, New Paltz
C. P. Lo, University of Georgia
Laurence J. C. Ma, University of Akron
Rhoads Murphey, University of Michigan
Marwyn Samuels, University of British Columbia
G. William Skinner, Stanford University
J. E. Spencer, University of California, Los Angeles (Emeritus)
Canute VanderMeer, University of Vermont
Joseph B. R. Whitney, University of Toronto
Wu Chuan-chun (Wu Chuanjun), Institute of Geography, Academia Sinica,
    Beijing

EDITORIAL STATEMENT

The CHINA GEOGRAPHER seeks to promote better understanding of
China through improved knowledge of its geography. To that end, we solicit
original manuscripts based on primary data that deal with various aspects
of China's physical and human geography. It is the policy of the editors and
publisher that each annual volume have a major theme and that all articles
relate to that theme. The 1981 volume (Number 11) focused on agriculture;
Number 12 (1984) focuses on China's environment. Each volume will also
contain relevant book reviews; although some of them will be solicited, we
also welcome contributed reviews.

Manuscripts should follow a consistent scientific system for the citation of references. We encourage a minimum of informational footnotes and request that authors employ *pinyin* romanization except where circumstances warrant otherwise. We also ask that authors follow the metric system of measurements. (A detailed stylesheet is available from the editors.) Material may be submitted to either Clifton W. Pannell or Christopher L. Salter, and correspondence regarding editorial policy, refereeing, and matters of style should be addressed to Clifton W. Pannell.

SUBSCRIPTIONS

The CHINA GEOGRAPHER is published by Westview Press. Correspondence concerning subscriptions should be addressed to the Subscription Manager, CHINA GEOGRAPHER, Westview Press, 5500 Central Avenue, Boulder, CO 80301.

Contents

Preface ix
Acknowledgements x
The Contributors xi

Management of Earthquake Hazard: The Program of Earthquake
Forecasting in China, 1966–1976, *Shiu-hung Luk* 1

The Effects of Forest on Water and Soil Conservation in the
Loess Plateau of China, *Liu Changming and Wu Kai* 25

Assessment of Potential Agricultural Land in Western
China with a Geographic Information System (GIS),
R. Welch, Yi-rong Hsu, and C. W. Pannell 39

The Changing Rural Landscape of China: A Study of Gaohe
Xian, Guangdong, *T. N. Chiu and C. K. Leung* 55

Urban Environmental Quality in China: A Luxury or a
Necessity? *Sen-dou Chang* 81

Water Resources Development and Its Environmental Impact on
Beijing, *Laurence J. C. Ma and Liu Changming* 101

Nature Preserves and Protected Wildlife in the People's
Republic of China, *Catherine S. Enderton* 117

Environmental Problems and the Development of Chinese
Fisheries, *Jaydee R. Hanson* 141

viii

Book Reviews

The Environment: Chinese and American Views,
edited by Laurence J. C. Ma and Allen Noble/
review by Ronald G. Knapp 157

South China in the Twelfth Century, A Translation of Lu Yu's
Travel Diaries, July 3-Dec. 6, 1170, translated and edited
by Chun-shu Chang and Joan Smythe/review by Joseph E.
Spencer 159

China's Island Frontier: Studies in the Historical Geography
of Taiwan, edited by Ronald Knapp/review by Joseph E. Spencer . . 162

China, A Geographical Survey, by T. R. Tregear/review by
Christopher L. Salter 165

Science in Contemporary China, edited by Leo A. Orleans/
review by Christopher L. Salter 168

Map Supplement

People's Republic of China, Nature Preserves and
Protected Wildlife, Catherine S. Enderton ....fold in

Preface

The last volume of the CHINA GEOGRAPHER (No. 11) "Agriculture" was inspired by the character and nature of much of the research work in geography going on in China. This tradition has continued, at least in part, here in Number 12 on China's environment. This number presents papers on a variety of environmental topics in China ranging from earthquake hazards to nature preserves. New data are displayed in descriptive, verbal, and tabular as well as cartographic form, and new research techniques and analytical methodologies are presented. Shiu-hung Luk begins the volume by examining the management of earthquake hazards through both traditional and new methods. His paper is followed by three studies focused on forest and agricultural land. The first of these is a quantitative modeling of the effect of forest growth on water and soil loss in a Loess Plateau study area. The authors—Liu Changming and Wu Kai—are from the Institute of Geography, Beijing. Roy Welch and colleagues use a geographic information system approach to evaluate agricultural land potential in the arid region around Urumqi, Xinjiang. A. R. T. N. Chiu and C. K. Leung describe the changing landscape of a rural xian not far from Canton based on their recent field studies there. There are two papers on city environments, Sen-dou Chang's general analysis and evaluation of urban environmental quality and Laurence Ma and Liu Changming's study of the development and environmental impact of water resources on the city of Beijing. Catherine Enderton has provided a full description of China's nature preserves and protected wildlife, and this article is accompanied by a map supplement. Jaydee Hanson discusses the relationship between environmental problems and the development of China's fisheries, a topic he has been investigating seriously for several years.

Five book reviews complete the volume. Ronald Knapp reviews a recent work on China's environment; Joseph Spencer reviews two works on China's historical geography; while Christopher Salter reviews a general geography text on China and a recent volume on science in contemporary China.

Clifton W. Pannell and Christopher L. Salter

Acknowledgements

The Editors wish to express thanks and to acknowledge the help of the following scholars for their time and expertise in reviewing manuscripts: Elgene Box, Sen-dou Chang, Ronnie J. Gilbert, Norton Ginsburg, John Hewlett, Laurence Ma, Rhoads Murphey, Kathleen Parker, G. William Skinner, Canute VanderMeer, Joseph B. R. Whitney, and Jack F. Williams. Anne Berryman deserves special thanks for her careful and exacting reviewing, copy-editing, and proofreading of the manuscripts and book reviews. Susan Haines took over for Anne Berryman in the late stages of production. She was very helpful in completing the editorial work and proofreading. Support for this number has come in many forms. Allen Noble and Teri Blount of the University of Akron were very patient and helpful with the typesetting. The Research Foundation at the University of Georgia and its director, Dr. Robert Anderson, Vice President for Research, were most generous in providing a grant for the costs of typesetting. The University of Georgia, Franklin College of Arts and Sciences and Department of Geography have continued to provide institutional support for which the editors are most grateful. Westview Press and its publisher Frederick Praeger and associate publisher Lynne Rienner have sustained their support for the *China Geographer*. We very much appreciate their continuing commitment to the study of China's geography.

C. W. P.
C. L. S.

The Contributors

Sen-dou Chang is Professor of Geography at the University of Hawaii, Manoa.

T. N. Chiu is Senior Lecturer in Geography, University of Hong Kong.

Catherine S. Enderton is completing her doctoral dissertation at the University of California, Los Angeles.

Jaydee R. Hanson is coordinator of the energy and environment program for the General Board of Church and Society of the United Methodist Church in Washington, D.C. He formerly analyzed developments in Asian fisheries for the National Marine Fisheries Service.

Ronald G. Knapp is Professor of Geography and Director of Asian Studies at the State University of New York at New Paltz.

Yi-rong Hsu is a Research Associate with the European Space Agency, Rome, Italy.

Liu Changming is Head, Department of Hydrology, Institute of Geography, Academia Sinica, Beijing.

C. K. Leung is Reader in Geography, University of Hong Kong.

Shiu-hung Luk is Assistant Professor of Geography, Erindale Campus, University of Toronto.

Laurence J. C. Ma is Professor of Geography and Director of International Programs at the University of Akron.

Clifton W. Pannell is Professor of Geography at the University of Georgia.

Christopher L. Salter is Associate Professor of Geography at the University of California, Los Angeles.

J. E. Spencer was Professor Emeritus of Geography at the University of California, Los Angeles.

R. A. Welch is Research Professor of Geography at The University of Georgia.

Wu Kai is a member of the Institute of Geography, Academia Sinica, Beijing.

Management of Earthquake Hazard: The Program of Earthquake Forecasting in China, 1966–1976

Shiu-hung Luk

INTRODUCTION

At five o'clock in the morning of March 8, 1966, a devastating earthquake of magnitude 6.8 struck a rural area near Xingtai, Hebei Province, 300 km southwest of Beijing. Damage was severe and widespread and many casualties were inflicted. The late Premier Zhou Enlai visited the area and immediately met with the leading earth scientists on his return to Beijing. As a result of these meetings, it was decided to embark on a "massive" program of earthquake forecasting.

In the evening of February 4, 1976, almost 10 years after the Xingtai event, a severe earthquake of magnitude 7.3 again struck, this time near the city of Haicheng, Liaoning Province. Damage to existing structures in the epicentral region was considerable, but, thanks to the accurate forecast of the event, massive evacuation of the local residents from their dwellings was effected and casualties were reduced to an insignificant number. This event, in fact, was the world's first major earthquake ever successfully forecasted. This

2

achievement was all the more remarkable considering the fact that the program of earthquake forecasting in China had been operating for less than 10 years.

Due to its success in preventing casualties, the Chinese program of earthquake forecasting attracted the attention of seismologists from many countries. An American delegation visited China in 1976 and reported on the successful forecast of the Haicheng event (HESD, 1977). Scientists from Japan (Suzuki, 1978a) and Mexico (Lomnitz and Lomnitz, 1978) obtained data on the forecasting of other Chinese earthquakes. These reports were mainly concerned with the technicalities of forecasting, as were most Chinese publications, while others (Gimenez, 1976; Bennett, 1979) dealt with the social aspect of earthquake prediction. Gimenez investigated the organization of the Chinese program and concluded that the different modes of social organization in China and the U.S. would likely have an enormous impact on structuring the possible social and economic consequences of earthquake predictions. Bennett evaluated the significance of mass participation in the program and considered that the amateur contribution was only of secondary importance.

The objectives of the present paper are twofold: to provide background to the initiation, design, and organization of the Chinese program and to evaluate the successes and failures of the program in the light of new information available regarding four major earthquakes which occurred in 1976. Gimenez (1976) commented on the scarcity of information available. The situation has not improved substantially in the past four years.

MAGNITUDE OF THE HAZARD

China possesses a unique earthquake record which dates back more than 3,000 years. Since the early 1950s a large team of scholars in the Chinese Academy of Sciences was organized to collate and interpret the records from numerous local gazetteer and history books. The intensity of each earthquake was assessed from the spatial variation of its reported severity, including sensing of shock waves, extent of damages, and observations of ground cracks as well as other geological changes. The magnitude of historical earthquakes was then established by comparing their isoseismal patterns with those of recent events.

The published record (CASGRI, 1976) shows that during the

period 780 B.C. to 1976 A.D.There were 656 earthquakes with a magnitude greater than 6.0,[1] or a frequency of approximately one in four years. In North China the record is virtually complete from about 1000 A.D. onward, as is illustrated by the linear relationship between earthquake magnitude and frequency (Hebei Province Seismological Bureau, 1977). The average frequency in this region is one in 15 years.

These average figures, however, do not reveal the uneven distribution of seismicity in space and time. In the seismicity map shown here (Figure 1), seismic 'zones' are located at the lithospheric plate boundary in a north-south belt at 103°E for 2,000 km. At 35°N the plate boundary runs east-west along the north slope of Qinling. Earthquake foci then follow two branches along deep-seated faults. A third branch runs from Haicheng southward for 1,200 km. Other seismic zones are found along mountainous belts in the west and the shelf areas near the island of Taiwan.

Seismicity in China is also unevenly distributed in time, with alternating periods of relative quiescence and activity. Each cycle of seismic activity begins with a quiescent period and culminates in massive energy releases during major earthquakes. These cycles have an average length of about 300 years in North China (Qiu, 1976) but are considerably shorter in many other regions (Deng et al., 1978).

In view of the high frequency of earthquakes, their uneven spatial and temporal distributions, the high population density, and the intensive land-use developed in China, it was inevitable that earthquakes had caused massive destruction. Listed in Table 1 are some of the severe earthquakes where casualties of greater than 10,000 were recorded. There were many others as described in published catalogues (Drake, 1912; CASGRI, 1976; Lee, Wu, and Jacobsen, 1976; Lee, Wu, and Wang, 1978), where damages were only described in qualitative terms. As shown in Table 1, the Haiyuan earthquake with a magnitude of 8.5 caused more than 200,000 casualties in 1920. The most devastating event ever recorded occurred in Shaanxi in 1556 with an estimated death toll of over 830,000. Such exceptionally high casualties obviously were not caused by the collapse of houses alone, but also by the incidences of fire, cold temperatures, starvation, and the lack of relief.

Since the founding of the People's Republic in 1949, major earthquakes have occurred in locations, including Xingtai in 1966; Luhuo in 1973; Haicheng in 1975; Tangshan in 1976; and in Longling, Songpan, and Yanyuan in 1976. During the Tangshan earthquake, which occurred in July 1976, most buildings in the City of Tangshan collapsed; 242,000 people perished; and 164,000 were

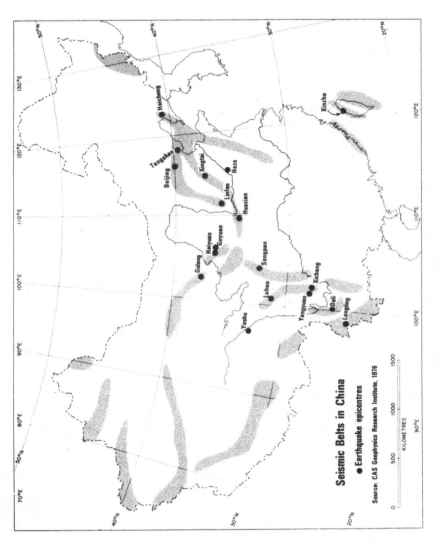

Figure 1. Seismic belts in China.

TABLE 1
Strong Earthquakes in China Since 1500 A.D.

Date	Location	Latitude[a]	Longitude[a]	Magnitude[a]	Intensity[a]	Casualties
Jan. 23, 1556	Huaxian, Shaanxi	34.5	109.7	8	11	>830,000[b]
Oct. 25, 1622	North of Guyuan, Ningxia	36.5	106.3	7	9-10	>20,000[c]
May 18, 1695	Linfen, Shanxi	36.0	111.5	8	10	>20,000[d]
Sept. 30, 1730	Western Suburb of Beijing	40.0	116.2	6½	>8	100,000[c]
1738	Yushu, Qinghai	33.0	97.0	6½	8	>50,000[b]
Sept. 12, 1850	Xichang, Sichuan	27.8	102.3	7½	10	15,000-20,000[c]
Dec. 16, 1920	Haiyuan, Ningxia	36.5	105.7	8½	12	>200,000[e]
Mar. 16, 1925	Dali, Yunnan	25.7	100.2	7	–	>10,000[f]
May 23, 1927	Gulang, Gansu	37.6	102.6	8	11	77,000[f]
Apr. 21, 1935	Xinzhu, Taiwan	24.5	120.8	7	10	15,255[g]
Aug. 1, 1937	Heze, Shandong	35.2	115.3	7	9	70,000[h]
July 28, 1976	Tangshan, Hebei	39.6	118.2	7.8	11	406,000[i]

[a] CASGRI (1976)

[b] Wang (1963, p. 24, 26)

[c] Drake (1912, p. 63)

[d] Meng and Lin (1977, p. 72)

[e] Fu (1976, p. 115)

[f] Deng (1937, p. 43)

[g] Wang (1967, p. 186)

[h] Tang Xiren (1978)

[i] Beijing Review, Dec. 7, 1979, No. 49, p. 7

seriously injured. This earthquake was so devastating that the City
of Tianjin, 100 km away, suffered a death toll of 10,000 (*South
China Morning Post*, 1976).

In the case of the Haicheng earthquake, which occurred in
February 1975, and which was successfully forecasted:

> "90% of the existing structures [in the City of
> Haicheng] were seriously damaged or destroyed; at
> Dingjiagou Brigade, 550 of the 700 buildings
> collapsed; at Shipengyu Brigade, 88% of the houses
> were destroyed; and at Shuiyuan Commune, 60 km
> from the epicentre, 820 of the 7,800 households were
> homeless after the earthquake, and 40% of the
> buildings were damaged. Including Haicheng
> [City],.....approximately one-half million people lived
> in this area, in which serious damage to or collapse
> of structures was at the 50% level. Hundreds of
> thousands of people must have been left homeless
> after the earthquake." (HESD, 1977, p. 243).

Casualties, however, were reported to be relatively few, and the
maximum death rate was 3.3 per 10,000 in the most heavily
damaged areas.[2] The contrast in casualty rates, due to these two
earthquakes, underscores the value of timely predictions and
warnings in averting potentially severe losses by injury or death
during earthquakes.

CHOICE OF ADJUSTMENTS TO THE HAZARD

Theoretically, there is a variety of possible human adjustments to
geophysical events such as earthquakes: affecting the cause,
modifying the loss potential, and bearing the losses (Burton, Kates,
and White, 1968). In reality, however, the range of choices for
adjustment is seldom available. In pre-Communist China, despite
early scientific advances, such as the invention of the first
seismograph in 132 A.D. (Needham, 1970, p. 627), the individual and
the nation as a whole had little choice but to bear the losses caused
by destructive earthquakes. Similarly, but under a different set of
circumstances in 1966, the Chinese Communist Party and the
Chinese Government had to face the challenge of demonstrating the
superiority of the new socialist system by preventing, or at least
reducing, damages caused by earthquakes. Since methods of
affecting the cause of earthquakes were (and still are) in their

embryo stage of development, modifying the loss potential was the only choice available. This may be achieved by the development of warning systems, by emergency evacuation, and by adopting appropriate quake-resistant building designs. In rural China houses of mud and masonry with heavy tile or mud roofs are very common, and they are vulnerable to collapse during earthquakes. To completely rebuild with stronger structures in hazardous areas was (and still is) economically infeasible. However, casualties might be prevented if the location, magnitude, and time of occurrence of earthquakes could be accurately predicted. Damaged areas could then be rebuilt with quake-resistant structures. It was within this context, therefore, that a massive program of earthquake forecasting was initiated in 1966, although it was far from certain at that point in time that earthquake forecasting was probable.

PROGRAM OF EARTHQUAKE FORECASTING

The Chinese program of earthquake forecasting is based on the detection of premonitors. It is generally known that earthquakes originate from the accumulation and sudden release of stresses set up by tectonic forces. Thus, detectable changes in the geophysical characteristics of the earth's crust, such as electrical resistivity, and surface expressions of the tectonic movements, such as ground tilt, can be expected. These detectable changes, along with some "response" phenomena, including changes in ground water quality and abnormal behavior of animals, have been employed by Chinese seismologists as earthquake premonitors. Because of the limited amount of data available and insufficient knowledge on the causes of the detectable changes, the magnitude, direction, as well as the temporal and spatial distribution pattern of these changes, cannot be specified. As a result, premonitors cannot be clearly isolated from noise. The only recourse is to monitor as many "premonitors" as possible with a dense network of observation points. Given the resource constraints on maintaining a dense network in all regions of the country, the forecasting program was optimized by assessing the general seismic risk of all regions and by providing a detailed monitoring network where results from the general assessment warranted it. In the earlier years of the program (1966–72), a system gradually evolved whereby seismic risks were assessed continuously, proceeding from general to very detailed monitoring. This process of assessment was conveniently divided into four stages: long-range,

8

medium-range, short-range, and imminent forecasting (Fang, 1979). The following discussion serves to illustrate the bases of these forecasts with special reference to the Haicheng and Tangshan earthquakes.

Long-Range Forecast

The long-range forecast, usually issued several years in advance, was largely based on the seismicity of a given geotectonic region. In most cases, the historical data available would indicate the current stage of seismicity (quiescent or active), and recent events, especially the spatial and temporal pattern of epicenter migration, would provide further indications. A case in point was in North China where three major events occurred between 1966 and 1969. If the spatial and temporal occurrence patterns were to continue, the next damaging earthquake could be within Liaoning Province (Figure 2). This was the principal reason why Liaoning Province was designated by the National Conference for Seismological Work in 1970 as an area deserving special seismological and geophysical attention (five years before the occurrence of the Haicheng earthquake). Subsequent to the designation, 17 new seismic stations were deployed, a releveling survey of the entire Liaotung Peninsula and adjacent regions was conducted, and other geophysical instruments were installed. Full-time geophysical personnel in the province rose from a few dozen workers to 300 (HESD, 1977).

Medium-Range Forecast

The strengthened monitoring program would provide geophysical data on the basis of which a medium-range forecast might be issued a few years to a few months in advance. In Liaoning Province, active uplift, intensified seismicity, and increased geomagnetic declination were observed. The State Seismological Bureau (SSB) thus concluded in June 1974 that a magnitude 5–6 earthquake might occur in the Bohai region within the next one or two years (HESD, 1977). Similarly, anomalous changes in gravity, geomagnetic intensity, telluric currents, ground electrical resistivity, radon concentration in ground water, and regional seismicity were observed in the Beijing-Tangshan region. In January 1976, six

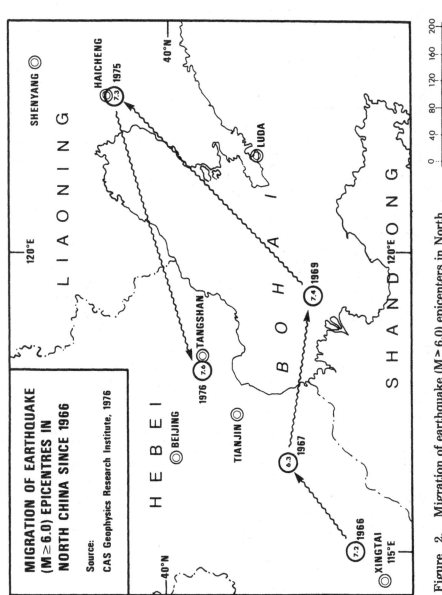

Figure 2. Migration of earthquake (M≥6.0) epicenters in North China since 1966.

10

months before the Tangshan event, the SSB issued a warning that an earthquake of magnitude 5–6 might occur in North Hebei (Wang, 1978).

Short-Range Forecast

Subsequent to the medium-range forecast stage, intensification of the monitoring program requires manpower which cannot be adequately supplied by the professional seismologists and, thus, amateurs, as well as the broad masses, are mobilized. As a result of the mobilization and the strengthening of the "anti-quake teams," the range of precursors monitored is expanded to include many "response" phenomena. All the geophysical, tectonic, as well as the "response" phenomena are evaluated in deciding the issuance of a short-range forecast. In Liaoning Province, changes in ground tilt, geomagnetism, water well systems, and animal behavior, as well as increases in radon emanation and telluric currents were reported since June 1974. On December 22, 1974, a swarm of earthquakes, the largest event being of magnitude 4.8, occurred 70 km northeast of Haicheng. All these phenomena were considered the forerunners of the major event. Thus, in January 1975, another SSB conference offered a short-term prediction that an earthquake of magnitude 5.5–6 would occur in the Yingkou-Luda-Tantung area in the first six months of 1975 (HESD, 1977). In Tangshan, no official short-term prediction was issued, although the Earthquake Observation Group of Gegongzhuang High School in Beijing offered the prediction on June 30, 1976, that an earthquake of a magnitude greater than 5 might occur near Tangshan in late July. This forecast was based on the group's observation of telluric currents (Wang, 1978). After the earthquake, which occurred July 28, 1976, analyses of available data showed that many premonitory phenomena did occur (Guo et al., 1977; Tanaka, 1978; Noritomi, 1978); but, unfortunately, they were considered insufficient evidences, and no warning was issued.

Imminent Forecast

Published information on the imminent forecasting of four major earthquakes in 1975-76 shows that the forecasts were based on the cumulative effect of the acceptable premonitors. At the same time, there is a remarkable variation in the strength of each premonitor (Table 2). In the case of the Haicheng earthquake, the increasing magnitude of a swarm of foreshocks, followed by about six hours of relative calmness, was considered the single most important precursor (Figure 3). Another clear precursor was the anomalous ground tilt followed by short-period pulses of telluric current. These observations, in conjunction with changes in the water table and water quality, abrupt emergence of artesian flow, and widespread reports of abnormal animal behavior, were considered sufficient evidence to issue an imminent forecast the morning of February 4, 1975 (HESD, 1977), nine hours before the occurrence of the earthquake. In contrast to the Haicheng event, the Songpan earthquake was forecasted despite the absence of foreshocks. The most significant anomalies cited were in radon emanation and telluric currents (Zhu and Jiang, 1978). Anomalies in radon concentration varied from +110% to −11% at five stations which were 40 to 320 km away from the epicenter. Of special note was the spike-like pattern at the Guzan station (Figure 4), which was observed six days before the first earthquake (M=7.2). Similar patterns were evident prior to earlier events which occurred along the same deep-seated fault in 1973 (Wakita, 1978). Another clear precursor was the large deviation followed by reversals in telluric currents recorded at five stations a few weeks before the major event (Noritomi, 1978). Other significant precursors include anomalies in geomagnetic intensity, ground water, animal behavior and, above all, increasing frequency of reports of flashes (Zhu and Jiang, 1978). The imminent warning was issued four days before the main event. In Tangshan some anomalies were observed shortly before the occurrence of the earthquake (Wang, 1978), but the collected information was not processed immediately because no short-range forecast was made. Thus, there was no possibility of providing adequate warning.

Participation of Professionals, Amateurs and the Broad Masses

From the above discussions, it is evident that a greater range of precursors, monitored by a denser network of observation points, was employed as the forecasting process intensified from the long-range to the imminent. This process of intensification was made possible by the policy of joining the efforts of specialists and amateur workers and working through the masses or mass

TABLE 2

Premonitors for the Imminent Forecast of
Four Severe Earthquakes in China, 1975-76

Premonitors	Haicheng[a] (Feb. 4, 1975)	Longling[b] (May 29, 1976)	Songpan[c] (Aug. 16, 1976)	Yanyuan[d] (Nov. 7, 1976)
Foreshock	VS	VS		VS
Crustal deformation	VS	S		S
Crustal Stress	S			S
Geomagnetism		S	S	VS-S
Telluric currents	VS	S	VS	S
Radon emanation	S	S	VS	S
Ground water	S	VS	S	S
Animal behavior	S	S	S	?
Others			S (flashes)	

VS: very significant; S: significant

[a]City of Yingkou (1976), HESD (1977)
[b]Tang, Chiyang (1978)
[c]Zhu and Jiang (1978)
[d]Noritomi (1978), Oike (1978), Tanaka (1978), Wakita (1978)

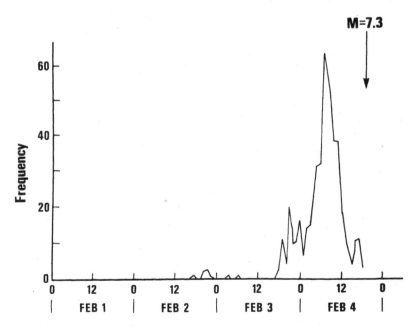

Figure 3. Frequency of foreshocks immediately before the Haicheng earthquake (after HESD, 1977).

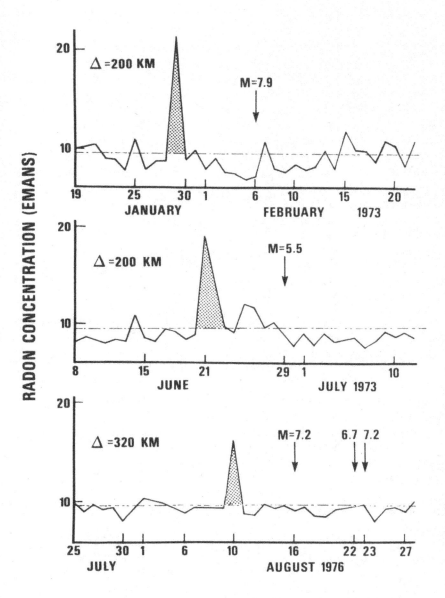

Figure 4. Precursor changes in the radon concentration in groundwater, Guzan, Sichuan (after Wakita, 1978).

participation. In China more than 5,000 qualified seismologists are employed by the State Seismological Bureau and Provincial Seismological Bureau and Brigades to operate 17 geophysical observatories and some 300 regional seismic stations. Another 5,000 workers with less technical training are employed to coordinate data-collection by amateurs (Jennings, 1980). The latter are volunteers who are organized as amateur groups in work units such as communes, brigades, factories, and schools. Each group is responsible to their respective local party committee and is also administratively attached to a seismic station from which some equipment and training are obtained. Both geophysical parameters and response phenomena are monitored by these groups. The number of amateur groups and observation points in a given area often varies with the known earthquake hazard. For instance, in the Haicheng area there were about 1,000 observation points in late 1974 (*Ta Kung Pao*, December 23, 1975), but when the short-range forecast of the earthquake was issued in mid-January, 1975, the number soared to more than 3,000 (*New China News Agency*, March 31, 1976). Generally, approximately 10,000 observation points are organized in provinces with a high seismic risk (Jennings, 1980). Because of the ad hoc nature of many observation points, some of the data collected by them may be of limited value. Suzuki (1978b) has commented on the low sensitivity of these data and the narrow concern by observers of relative anomaly regardless of absolute values. However, the quality of data collected at many observation points has improved over a period of time, so that they contributed significantly to accurate forecasts. A case in point was the observation of anomalies in telluric currents at Shenyang Middle School Number 13 on the day of the Haicheng earthquake (HESD, 1977, p. 248).

One of the major contributions of the broad masses who participated in the program of earthquake forecasting was their monitoring of response phenomena such as the abnormal behavior of animals. With a minimal amount of instructions, rural folk in particular, who are in frequent contact with animals and wells, and who work outdoors, can easily recognize abnormalities. The abnormalities are then reported to their respective work units and relayed to seismic stations. Many of the response phenomena are folk wisdom, now considered by Chinese seismologists as valid precursors. Here only abnormal animal behavior is discussed. In the early 1970s, when the Chinese program became known, western scientists were very skeptical of the validity of using animal behavior to predict earthquakes. It was not publicized then that, since 1968, six experimental stations were established in Hebei Province and Xinjiang Uygur Autonomous Region to investigate the relationships between behavior of 10 kinds of animals including pigeons and cats, and the incidence of medium-magnitude $(3 < M < 5)$ earthquakes (CASBRI, 1977; Anhui Seismological Bureau, 1978; Shen, 1978). One result of the experiments shows that the association between abnormal behavior of pigeons and the occurrence of earth tremors is statistically significant. The apparent explanation of this association is that pigeons possess some 100 tiny units between the leg's tibia and fibula which are connected to the nerve center and are very sensitive to mechanical vibrations. Shortly before the occurrence of major earthquakes in 1975 and 1976, abnormal behavior of animals was widely observed in the epicentral regions, and these observations were considered to be of significance in the issuance of imminent forecasts (Table 2). Outside China the use of abnormal animal behavior as a precursor has not yet been accepted fully. However, it is being considered seriously, and validation studies are being conducted in the United States (Otis and Kantz, 1979).

EVALUATION OF THE PROGRAM

Obviously, the best way to evaluate the program is to consider the number of correct forecasts relative to the total number of predictions. Unfortunately, the available record is incomplete. Oike (1978) listed 29 imminent forecasts made between 1967 and 1976, but many of them only applied to local areas. There are probably many other false alarms, as suggested by U.S. and Japanese scientists who visited China, but the total number is not known. Alternatively, it is possible to consider the number of major events correctly forecasted. In 1975 and 1976, five major earthquakes of magnitude ≥ 7.0 occurred, and four of them (Table 2) were correctly predicted. This is a fairly high success rate if false alarms are disregarded. Casualties and some damage to properties were prevented by these forecasts. Unfortunately, the most destructive event—the Tangshan earthquake—was not predicted. The Tangshan earthquake inflicted a record number of casualties since the Huaxian earthquake of 1556 (Table 1). Why then were the four major earthquakes successfully forecasted and yet the most potentially destructive of them all was not forecasted?

Judging from the type of premonitors employed, it is quite clear that the successes were not achieved by any technological breakthrough. The geophysical and tectonic parameters monitored are the same ones measured in the United States and Japan. The only exceptions are the "response" phenomena such as ground water quality and abnormal behavior of animals, but the use of these response phenomena can hardly be considered a technological breakthrough since a considerable number of western scientists are still skeptical of their status as premonitors. Hence, it is only logical to suggest that at least part of the success should be attributed to the policy of mass participation. Through mass participation, many more stations and observation points can be maintained. This is clearly of the utmost importance since the expected characteristics of premonitors are poorly defined at the present state of the art of earthquake forecasting, and only a limited number of professional seismologists are available.

At the same time, there are other advantages with the policy of mass participation. Because of the large number of people who participated in the program, practically every community in the hazard area is involved. General public awareness of the hazard is thus substantially heightened. Such awareness would facilitate the dissemination of general knowledge on earthquakes by publicity teams organized by party committees and related government agencies. It would also motivate the local planning of emergency evacuation. The successful public education campaigns and detailed planning of emergency evacuation in China were considered crucial in effectively reducing casualties and other damages during earthquakes (City of Yingkou, 1976). The decision to issue an earthquake warning is made by repeated consultations among local, regional, provincial, and national units, brigades and bureaus, thus allowing considerable input by the local communities in the decision-making process. It is no wonder that public compliance to earthquake warning was reported to be excellent. Evacuations were always orderly and promptly carried out and false alarms were met with few complaints (Gimenez, 1976; City of Yingkou, 1976). In general, the adoption of the mass participation policy is instrumental in resolving some of the social problems that militate against successful earthquake forecasting.

Another factor which contributes to the success of the program relates to the permissible range of the three elements of forecasting: time, place, and magnitude, which to a large extent determine the feasibility of forecasting. In terms of place, large areas are covered by imminent forecasts in China. For instance, the imminent alarm for the Longling earthquake covers about a quarter of the area of Yunnan Province, which encompasses 100,000 km^2. For occurrence time, imminent forecasts in China usually cover a few days, as did the forecasts for the major events of Songpan and Yanyuan. Forecasts of magnitude in China are issued with a range of one-half or one unit of magnitude. This range is considerable because the magnitude scale used is logarithmic. Thus, for all the three elements of forecasting, the permissible range is quite large when compared with the requirements in Japan or the United States (Suzuki, 1978b). This is justified in the case of China because seismic risks are higher, potential damage is heavier, and erroneous forecasts incur relatively fewer costs. Even if the erroneous forecasts are disregarded, the program of earthquake forecasting has not been a total success due to the failure to predict the most destructive event—the Tangshan earthquake. The cause of this failure is still not fully known, but information gathered by U.S. and Japanese scientists who visited China in the last few years provides some plausible answers.

First, the Chinese efforts were based almost entirely on empirical evidences with very limited theoretical support. Because of the use of empiricism over theory, the causes of the premonitions are not fully understood. Therefore, it is not possible to specify the characteristics of the premonitors even if the event is duplicated in the same geotectonic region. A case in point relates to the differences in the premonitors between the Haicheng and the Tangshan earthquakes, which were both located in the North China geotectonic region (Figure 2). The substantial differences in seismicity, as well as the occurrence time of ground and animal behavior anomalies (Figure 5) show clearly the difficulty of transferring experience in forecasting. Such differences could have contributed significantly to the failure to predict the Tangshan earthquake, which occurred 17 months after the Haicheng event.

Second, many available premonitors show inconsistent areal patterns in the Tangshan region. For instance, some stations, especially the one at Chengli, showed clear indications of abnormality in the electrical resistivity readings immediately before the earthquake, but other stations located closer to the epicenter showed no corresponding abnormality (Wang, 1978). Similar inconsistencies are found for a number of premonitors. Clearly, this is a question of how to isolate the "sensitive" stations from the "noise," and it is certainly not a simple task considering the fact that only four out of 1,000 wells studied in Yunnan Province are

18

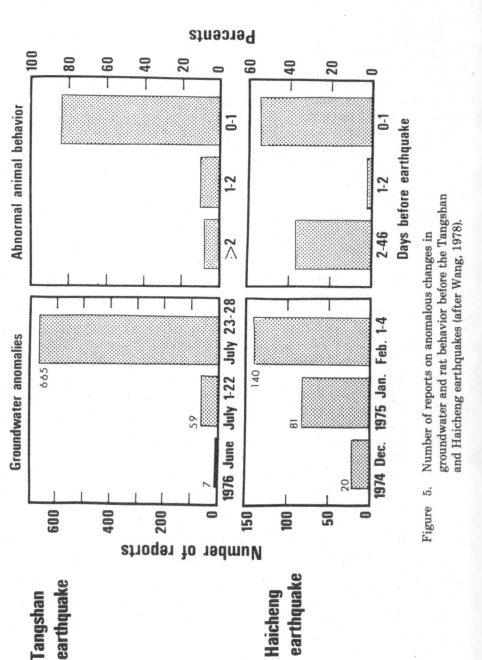

Figure 5. Number of reports on anomalous changes in groundwater and rat behavior before the Tangshan and Haicheng earthquakes (after Wang, 1978).

labeled useful for forecasting (Wakita, 1978). At present there appears to be no satisfactory method other than simple trial-and-error. In Sichuan observations prior to earthquakes, which occurred before 1976, provided opportunities to identify these sensitive stations and thus contributed to the successful forecasts. The lack of this experience in Tangshan must have substantially reduced the chances of predicting this event.

Third, Wang (1978) and many others, ascribed the failure of predicting the Tangshan earthquake to the lack of foreshocks. This is certainly a factor to bear in mind, but it is not necessarily the principal factor. The Songpan event demonstrates the possibility of a successful forecast without foreshocks. Also, it is generally known that only half of severe earthquakes are heralded by moderately strong foreshocks (Kerr, 1978), and there is no doubt that the Chinese seismologists were aware of that. Even if foreshocks had occurred a few days before the major event, they only could have alerted some seismologists who would not have been allowed enough time to organize the anti-quake teams, establish mass observation points, process the data on premonitors, and issue timely warnings.

On the whole, the principal cause of the failure to predict is the nature of the forecasting method itself. For the Tangshan event, it was not only a failure to provide timely warnings; in the larger perspective it was also a failure to establish the causes of the premonitions. Lomnitz and Lomnitz (1978) rightly suggested that the Tangshan earthquake could not have been predicted at the present state of the art of forecasting. Similar failures to predict major earthquakes will continue to occur unless understanding of the mechanisms that trigger earthquakes and causes of the observed premonitions can be substantially improved.

DISCUSSION AND CONCLUSION

In view of the nature of earthquakes and the extent of our knowledge on earthquakes, the two-pronged approach of combining professional and mass efforts adopted in the earthquake forecasting program in China is clearly justified. Studies of earthquake and other hazard warning systems in the United States (Mileti, 1975; White and Haas, 1975) show that there are serious constraints to these systems unless the forecasts are perfectly accurate. These constraints largely relate to the economic and social havoc that will follow a false alarm. The costs involved in case of an erroneous forecast may exceed potential damages. In China these problems are less serious, not only because of the vastly different system of social organization, which favors discipline and group consciousness, but also because of the successful public education campaigns and a high level of mass participation in the forecasting program. This is not to suggest that false alarms do not bear economic and social costs in China but this suggests that the costs involved are far more tolerable than the casualties inflicted by destructive earthquakes.

Several authors have commented on the role of mass participation in the program of earthquake forecasting in China. Bennett (1979) recognized that the amateur network and mass organizations "are an integral part of the observation network, contributing types and amounts of data that are simply beyond the limited reach of the specialists alone, even if this data is judged by the professionals to vary enormously in quality" (p. 107). He then concluded that "the amateur contribution is real though clearly secondary" (Bennett, 1979, p. 106). There is little doubt that only some of the collected information by the amateurs is useful for earthquake forecasting. However, apart from providing data and extending the network of observation points, the amateurs and the masses also exerted a strong positive influence on the mass education campaigns, the execution of emergency evacuation plans, and the public compliance to warnings. Seen in this light, the total contribution by the amateurs was very substantial, and mass participation should be considered of primary significance in the earthquake forecasting program. To this author, it is very doubtful whether the forecasting of the four major earthquakes which occurred in 1975-76, as well as the prevention of serious damages from these earthquakes, could have been possible without the participation of the masses.

The Chinese program of earthquake forecasting was initiated in 1966 but was not really underway until the late 1960s. In less than a decade, it has proven to be instrumental in reducing a substantial amount of losses due to earthquakes. In particular, China made the world's first accurate forecast of a major earthquake in 1975 and managed to predict four out of five major earthquakes which occurred in 1975 and 1976. In this regard, the program should be considered fairly successful. However, some qualifications to this evaluation should be added. The methods used for forecasting were highly empirical, in most cases not scientifically vigorous, and in many respects qualitative and subjective. The infrequent use of statistical methods to establish the significance of anomalous readings (Suzuki, 1978b; Qian and Zhou, 1980) serves to illustrate the inadequacy of the forecasting method. The difficulty of isolating sensitive data and stations from noise due to an imperfect understanding of the detailed causes of earthquake premonition, is the principal reason why the very destructive Tangshan earthquake was not predicted. Without a substantial improvement in our knowledge of earthquake premonition and earthquake-triggering mechanisms, similar failures will definitely occur in the future. Incidentally, recent Chinese publications (e.g., Wu, Wang, and Li, 1980) indicate that some effort is being made to extend our knowledge in these areas. It is hoped that this effort will be sustained for a sufficiently long period of time and that earthquake forecasting will become increasingly more reliable in the near future.

NOTES

1. Lee, Wu, and Wang (1978) cited a number of earthquakes in Taiwan not included in the list published by the Chinese Academy of Sciences. Therefore, the total number of known historical earthquakes should be more than 656.

2. A brief report on the work of the meritorious units cited by the State Council of the People's Republic of China for earthquake observation and prediction in the southern region of Liaoning Province. *Earthquake Frontiers*, Vol. 2, 2-3. (Cited in Gimenez, 1976).

LITERATURE CITED

Anhui Province Seismological Bureau, 1978, *Macroscopic Anomalies and Earthquakes*. Beijing: Seismology Press, (in Chinese).

Beijing Review, 1979, (December 7), No. 49, p. 7.

Bennett, Gordon, 1979, Mass campaigns and earthquakes: Hai-Ch'eng, 1975. *China Quarterly*, No. 77, 94-112.

Burton, Ian, R.W. Kates and Gilbert White, 1968, *The Human Ecology of Extreme Geophysical Events*. Natural Hazard Research Working Paper No. 1. Toronto: Department of Geography, University of Toronto.

Chinese Academy of Sciences, Biophysics Research Institute (CASBRI), 1977, *Animals and Earthquakes*. Beijing: Seismology Press, (in Chinese).

Chinese Academy of Sciences, Geophysics Research Institute (CASGRI), 1976, *Abbreviated List of Strong Earthquakes ($M \geq 6.0$) in China*. Beijing: Map Publishers, (in Chinese).

City of Yingkou, 1976, *Southern Liaoning Earthquake*. Beijing: Commercial Press, (in Chinese).

Deng, Qidong, Yuming Zhang, Wenlin Huan, Hongsheng Zhang, Guilin Hu, Yiming Liu, Ruisheng Deng, Qun Li, Xingsong Liu, Tianxi Yang, Futian Fan, 1978, Major characteristics of seismicity and seismo-geology in China. *Science Bulletin*, Vol. 23, 193-199, (in Chinese).

Deng, Yun-te, 1937, *A History of Natural Disaster Relief in China*. Second Impression, 1970. Taipei: Commercial Press, (in Chinese).

Drake, N.F., 1912, Destructive earthquakes in China. *Bulletin, Seismological Society of America*, Vol. 2, 40-91.

Fang, Weiqing, 1979, Progress of earthquake prediction research in China. *Acta Geophysica Sinica*, Vol. 22, 351-357, (in Chinese).

Fu, Chengyi, 1976, *Ten Chapters on Earth Sciences*. Beijing: Science Publishers, (in Chinese).

Gimenez, M.E., 1976, A "people's war" against earthquakes: lessons from the Chinese experience with earthquake prediction. *Mass Emergencies*, Vol. 1, 323-341.

Guo, Shunmin, Zhiyi Li, Shaoping Cheng, Xiancheng Chen, Xiaode Chen, Zhuen Yang, and Rucheng Li, 1977, Discussion of the regional structural background and the seismogenic model of the Tangshan earthquake. *Scientia Geologica Sinica*, No. 4, 305-321, (in Chinese).

Haicheng Earthquake Study Delegation (HESD), 1977, Prediction of the Haicheng earthquake. *EOS, Transactions, American Geophysical Union*, Vol. 58, 236-272.

Hebei Province Seismological Bureau, 1977, On the earthquake risk of the Hebei Province of North China. *Acta Geophysica Sinica*, Vol. 20, 232-241, (in Chinese).

Jennings, P.C., editor, 1980, *Earthquake Engineering and Hazard Reduction in China*. Washington, D.C.: National Academy of Sciences.

Kerr, R.A., 1978, Earthquakes: prediction proving elusive. *Science*, Vol. 200, 419-421.

Lee, W.H.K., F.T. Wu and Carl Jacobsen, 1976, A catalogue of historical earthquakes in China compiled from recent Chinese publications. *Bulletin, Seismological Society of America*, Vol. 66, 2,003-2,016.

_____ , _____ and S.C. Wang, 1978, A catalogue of instrumentally determined earthquakes in China (magnitude$\geq$6) compiled from various sources. *Bulletin, Seismological Society of America*, Vol. 68, 383-398.

Lomnitz, C. and L. Lomnitz, 1978, Tangshan 1976: a case history in earthquake prediction. *Nature*, Vol. 271, 109-111.

Meng, Fenxing and Hongwen Lin, 1977, On using ancient buildings and other cultural relics to study some aspects of two major historical earthquakes in Shanxi. In *Earthquakes and Archaeological Studies of Earthquakes*. Beijing: Culture Press, pp. 51-91, (in Chinese).

Mileti, D.S., 1975, *Natural Hazard Warning Systems in the United States: A Research Assessment*. Boulder: Institute of Behavioral Science, University of Colorado, Boulder.

New China News Agency, 1976, (March 31).

Needham, Joseph, 1970, *Science and Civilization in China, Vol. 3, Mathematics and the Sciences of the Heavens and the Earth.* London: Cambridge University Press.

Noritomi, Kazuo, 1978, Application of precursory geoelectric and geomagnetic phenomena to earthquake prediction in China. *Chinese Geophysics*, Vol. 1, 377-392.

Oike, K., 1978, Precursory phenomena and prediction of recent large earthquakes in China. *Chinese Geophysics*, Vol. 1, 179-200.

Otis, L.S. and W.H. Kantz, 1979, *Biological premonitors of earthquakes: a validation study.* Paper presented at the International Symposium on Earthquake Prediction, Paris, April.

Qian, Shangwei and Yongming Zhou, 1980, Statistical analysis of the imminent earthquake anomalies discriminant. *Acta Geophysica Sinica*, Vol. 23, 219-231, (in Chinese).

Qiu, Qun, 1976, The tectonic background of the Tangshan earthquake of July 28, 1976, Hebei Province, and its activity. *Acta Geophysica Sinica*, Vol. 19, 259-269, (in Chinese).

Shen, Ling-huang, 1978, Can animals help to predict earthquakes? *Earthquake Information Bulletin*, Vol. 10, No. 6, 231-233.

South China Morning Post, 1976, (August 20), p. 22.

Suzuki, Ziro, 1978a, General introduction to the China visit by the delegation of the Seismological Society of Japan in 1977. *Chinese Geophysics*, Vol. 1, 173-177.

———— , 1978b, On the Chinese prediction of earthquakes. *Chinese Geophysics*, Vol. 1, 393-399.

Ta Kung Pao, 1975, (December 23).

Tanaka, Yutaka, 1978, Reports on observations of crustal stress and crustal deformation, and their anomalous changes related to earthquakes in China. *Chinese Geophysics*, Vol. 1, 425-442.

Tang, Chiyang, 1978, Bases for the prediction of the Lungling earthquake and the temporal and spatial characteristics of precursors. *Chinese Geophysics*, Vol. 1, 400-424.

Tang, Xiren, 1978, *History of Earthquakes in China.* Beijing: Science Press, (in Chinese).

Wakita, Hiroshi, 1978, Earthquake prediction and geochemical studies in China. *Chinese Geophysics*, Vol. 1, 443-457.

Wang, C.Y., 1978, Some aspects of the Tangshan (China) earthquake of 1976. *Chinese Geophysics*, Vol. 1, 157-172.

Wang, Jiayin, 1963, *Historical Sources on the Geology of China.* Beijing: Science Press, (in Chinese).

Wang, Jing-liang, 1967, Earthquake hazards in Taiwan. In *Natural Hazards in Taiwan*, Taiwan Research Bulletin No. 95. Taiwan: Economics Research Unit, The Bank of Taiwan, pp. 170-214, (in Chinese).

White, G.F. and J.E. Haas, 1975, *Assessment of Research on Natural Hazards.* Cambridge, Mass.: MIT Press.

Wu, Jinxiu, Yaling Wang, and Shengyong Li, 1980, The characteristics of forerunner field of underground water regime during the Tangshan earthquake and its focal evolution process. *Seismology and Geology*, Vol. 2, 65–78, (in Chinese).

Zhu, Jiezuo and Zaixiong Jiang, 1978, *The Songpan Earthquake*. Beijing: Seismology Press, (in Chinese).

The Effects of Forest on Water and Soil Conservation in the Loess Plateau of China

Liu Changming
Wu Kai

INTRODUCTION

It has been estimated that the annual sediment transportation, in terms of suspended load in China's rivers, exceeds 2,600,000,000 metric tons (Editorial Committee, 1981), of which the amount delivered by the Yellow River is the highest, being 1,600,000,000 metric tons (Table 1). The sediment in the Yellow River comes mainly from the Loess Plateau in the middle reaches of the Yellow River. The amount of sediment transported between Hekouzhen and Shaanxian is 90 percent of the total sediment yield in Shaanxian. In this region the annual average soil erosion module exceeds 5,000 $t/km^2/yr$, with maximum value of 34,500 $t/km^2/yr$ observed in the Wuding River basin located on the Loess Plateau in north Shaanxi Province (Figure 1).

Thus, in terms of harnessing the Yellow River by means of afforestation as well as soil conservation, sediment reduction has become a matter of common concern. It is also an interesting research topic for geographers and hydrologists.

In order to ascertain the role of afforestation as an effective measure of water and soil conservation, we carried out a preliminary

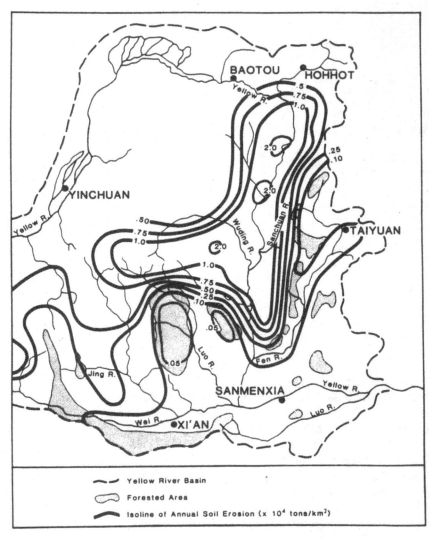

Figure 1. Distribution of forested areas and soil erosion in the middle reaches of the Yellow River

TABLE 1

Average Annual Sediment Transportation of the Major Rivers in China

River	Station	Area (km^2)	Average annual sediment transportation (1,000 t)	Erosion modules ($t/km^2/yr$)	Years of observation
Huanghe	Lanzhou	222,551	119,000	534	1935–70
	Hekouzhen	385,966	167,000	451	1952–70
	Hekouzhen Shaanxian	301,903	1,433,000	4,801	
	Shaanxian	687,869	1,600,000	2,330	1919–59
Liaohe	Tielin	120,764	20,980	173	1959–70
Luanhe	Luanxian	44,100	24,080	546	1956–70
Yongdinhe	Guanting	42,500	80,700	1,686	1925–52
Huaihe	Bengbu	121,330	13,080	107	1956–70
Chang-jiang	Datong	1,705,383	499,600	293	1956–70
Xijiang	Wuzhou	329,705	66,490	201	1956–70

investigation to study the effects of forest on sediment reduction and to assess the effectiveness of various measures adopted for soil conservation on the Loess Plateau. It is well known that water conservation and soil conservation are very effective in the control of water loss and soil erosion in small watersheds, but the effectiveness of water and soil conservation in medium and large river basins has not been ascertained because of lack of research. In addition, the feasibility of transforming the loessland on a large scale by revegetation has become an issue. Central to the issue has been what would happen to the regional economy that for years has been based almost entirely on the growth of grains. This issue, when resolved, is likely to affect the policy of harnessing the Yellow River and the future direction of soil conservation work in the Loess Plateau region.

Soil conservation work has been conducted in the loess region for more than two decades, yet it has not shown much apparent effect on the control of flooding and sedimentation in the mainstream of the Yellow River. Therefore, some people are no longer convinced that successful water and soil conservation in this region is possible. For this reason, our experimental data observed at the Huanglong Experimental Station in northern Shaanxi Province can be taken as a basis to study the effectiveness of forest on soil and water conservation. At the same time we also conducted similar research in selected large forested river basins. Our ultimate purpose in doing these two separate and yet interrelated research projects is to predict the effect of afforestation on water and soil conservation. Such a prediction can also be of value in solving the problem of harnessing the Yellow River.

PHYSICAL BACKGROUND

The Loess Plateau of China is the largest such plateau in the world. It is distributed in north China and has an area of about 600,000 km^2 with an average depth of loess of more than 50 m. It is bordered by Inner Mongolia to the north, the Qinling Mountains to the south, the Qilian Mountains to the west, and the Taihang Mountains to the east. The following provinces are included in this region: all of Shanxi, most parts of Shaanxi and Gansu, and the Ningxia Hui Autonomous Region. The Yellow River and its many tributaries such as the Taohe, Weihe, Luohe, Jinghe, and Fenhe flow through the Loess Plateau, and the loess that they carry has a great influence on the Yellow River's hydrology.

Generally speaking, in this area the elevations west of the Liupan Mountains are mostly about 2,000 m above sea level, and to the east of the Liupan Mountains they are between 1,000–2,000 m. The middle reaches of the Yellow River have the thickest loess deposits. In the Huajialing and Mahan Mountains in Gansu Province, the thickness of the loess varies between 200–300 m. These are believed to be the thickest loess deposits in the world. Between the Liupan and the Luliang Mountains in north Shaanxi and west Shanxi the thickness ranges between 100–200 m. Outside of the aforementioned area in the middle reaches of the Yellow River the loess deposits are thin. The river's middle reaches are located in the region where the loess cover is the deepest. The thick loess is eroded by intensive rainstorms and produces a large amount of sediment material for the Yellow River.

The major landforms of the best developed loess areas in the middle reaches of the Yellow River can be classified into three kinds: *yuan*, *liang*, and *mao*. The *yuan* is a highland (high table-like) plain with abrupt edges descending to valleys. The surface of the *yuan* is very flat, having a slope of less than 50 percent, which is suitable for farming. The *liang* is an elongated loess mound and has an arched top with smooth slopes along its major axis. It always lies between two valleys. The *mao* is a round loess mound and has steep slopes on all sides with many gullies. The erosion of the loess has the following sequences. After a *yuan* has been dissected by valleys, it is turned into several *liang*. A *liang*, in turn, can be cut by gullies and becomes several *mao*. Thus the occurrence of many *mao* means that the soil erosion in a region is very severe. *Mao* are now widely distributed in north Shaanxi and northwestern Shanxi, covering an area of about 57,000 km^2 (Gong and Jiang, 1979).

According to Chinese historical records, the Loess Plateau 3,000 years ago was a wooded area with a forest coverage of about 53 percent. After a long period of deforestation, woodland accounted for only 3 percent of the Loess Plateau in 1949. The remaining wooded regions are mainly concentrated in the Ziwuling and the Huanglong mountainous areas in the basins of the Beiluo River and Jing River, both tributaries of the Yellow River. For example, the forest coverage ratio amounts to 47.6 percent in the area upstream from the Zhuangtou Hydrological Station in the Beiluo River Basin, which has an area of 25,165 km^2. Due to thousands of years of deforestation in most areas of the Loess Plateau, vegetation cover is

TABLE 2

Relationship Between Sediment Volume and Forest Coverage Ratio in the Loess Plateau

Geomor-phologic region	Hydrological station	Forest coverage ratio (%)	Annual sed. tran. modules Me (t/km^2)	Soil erosion by rainfall Ep (t/km^2/mm)	Soil erosion by runoff Er (t/km^2/mm)
Mao	Liujiahe	18.3	8,720	19.73	344
	Gedong Houtongcheng	21.9	6,930	13.44	128
	Average of 20 gullies	0	13,500	36.20	620
Mao and liang	Zhangcunyi	97.0	64	0.12	4
	Banqiao	67.1	819	1.52	54
	Dacun	62.8	1,150	2.19	30
	Ganguyi	13.0	7,290	17.50	232
	Jiaokouhe-Zhangcunyi-Liujiahe	73.8	769	1.44	32
	Yueyue	2.1	7,200	21.74	283
	Yueyue-Qingyang	11.5	6,520	13.67	274
	Average of 11 gullies	0	8,725	23	320

very sparse, and serious soil erosion occurs as a result of frequent rainstorms that are heavily concentrated in the summer months under the influence of the monsoon.

METHODOLOGY

One of the approaches widely adopted by hydrologists to investigate the influence of forest upon watershed hydrology is the Paired Catchment Method (Hewlett, 1981, pp. 67–80). This comparative method uses two nearby watersheds, one with forest cover and the other without, where the physicogeographical conditions are similar. The hydrological characteristics of the two watersheds are then comparatively gauged during a calibration period, after which the forest on one basin is altered experimentally. On the basis of the Paired Catchment Method we developed a methodology which has proved to be useful.

It is well known that runoff and sediment conditions are related to forest growth. We have collected extensive experimental data in the loess region of China which reveal that surface runoff and sediment yield are always an inverse function of forest coverage. This relationship can be mathematically described by multinomial equations. Using y for runoff or for sediment values and x for forest growth characteristics, we have a general equation as follows:

$$y = a \pm bx \pm cx^2 \pm \dots \pm kx^n \tag{1}$$

where a, b, c,...k are coefficients. Obviously, equation (1) expresses the nonlinear relationship of y versus x. In such a case the solution can be obtained by calculating n simultaneous equations:

$$y_1 = a_1 \pm b_1 x \pm c_1 x^2 \pm \dots \pm k_1 x^n$$
$$y_2 = a_2 \pm b_2 x \pm c_2 x^2 \pm \dots \pm k_2 x^n$$
$$\dots\dots\dots\dots\dots\dots\dots\dots\dots\dots\dots\dots\dots \tag{2}$$
$$\dots\dots\dots\dots\dots\dots\dots\dots\dots\dots\dots\dots\dots$$
$$y_n = a_n \pm b_n x \pm c_n x^2 \pm \dots \pm k_n x^n$$

The solution to these equations seems to be easy, but in fact it is very difficult in finding n comparable watersheds with the same physicogeographical conditions. Fortunately, we have found that the number of items (n) in equation (2) is generally limited to three. For instance, the equation for annual runoff versus forest coverage has three items only (Liu, 1981). Therefore, equations (2) become:

$$y_1 = a_1 \pm b_1 x \pm c_1 x^2$$
$$y_2 = a_2 \pm b_2 x \pm c_2 x^2 \qquad (3)$$
$$y_3 = a_3 \pm b_3 x \pm c_3 x^2$$

The solutions to these equations (3) require three comparative watersheds. According to our analysis of the observed data of the loess region, the linear relationship between surface runoff and forest coverage can be assumed. Thus, equations (2) can be simplified as follows:

$$y_1 = a_1 \pm b_1 x$$
$$y_2 = a_2 \pm b_2 x \qquad (4)$$

Equations (4) show that the solution is very easy, requiring only two watersheds for comparative analysis. In such a case, the aforementioned Paired Catchment Method is in line with equations (4), which can be seen as a special case of equations (2). In other words, the Paired Catchment Method is suitable for the analysis of the linear relationship between hydrological value and forest growth characteristics.

In order to quantitatively analyze the influence of forest on water loss and on soil erosion, the aforementioned simultaneous equations were used in our research as a more flexible and yet precise method to assess the impact of forest coverage on runoff and sediment yield. This quantitative approach is more applicable than the paired method, which quite often suffers from the difficulty of finding a pair of comparable watersheds. Moreover, the Paired Catchment Method, as an experimental method, was developed under a controlled condition in which one watershed was fully forested while the other was entirely devoid of trees. Our method is not limited by such constraints. It can be easily employed to study the effects of any partial forest coverages on soil and water conservation. It can also be used to estimate such an effect in a watershed under full forest cover on the basis of the data from a partially forested watershed nearby.

THE EFFECT OF FOREST ON WATER AND SOIL CONSERVATION

According to the experimental data and statistics of seven large and medium sized river basins with similar physicogeographic conditions, which we selected for comparative analysis in the forest region of the Loess Plateau, the effect of forest on the reduction of flood (surface water) is proportional to forest coverage, (i.e., their relationship is linear). When the forest coverage ratio reaches 100 percent, the effectiveness of the forest on the reduction of floodwater amounts to 90 percent or so, regardless of the sizes of the watersheds. Forest growth also diminishes the peak discharge by 70-95 percent. The effect of forest on peak discharge in large basins seems to be slightly less than that in small watersheds.

The forest cover in the Loess Plateau has a negative effect on annual runoff. This problem has been dealt with in another paper by the senior author (Liu, 1981), so we will not repeat it here.

In order to study the effect of forest on the reduction of sediment product, 39 small watersheds with different forest coverage ratios on the Loess Plateau were selected. Some of the watersheds are covered with natural forests while others are located in afforested regions. The observed data of those watersheds in terms of annual sediment transportation, the annual sediment transportation module (Me in $t/km^2/yr$) and the annual soil erosion (Ep, Er) are processed and given in Table 2. Soil erosion, Ep, is the Me divided by precipitation and soil erosion, Er, equals to Me divided by runoff. Thus the units of Ep and Er are in $t/km^2/yr/mm$. From Table 2 the apparent relationship between the Me and forest coverage ratio (x) can be fixed. The greater is the forest coverage ratio, the less is the annual sediment transportation module (Me). In other words, the annual soil erosion (Ep, Er) in the basins decreases with the increase of forest coverage ratio (x).

The correlation curves of Me, Ep, Er versus x were plotted. They showed that the Me, Ep, and Er decreased with maximum rate in the beginning when x starts to increase, and they became stabilized when x had a high ratio, (i.e., the relationships between x and Me, Ep and Er are nonlinear). However, these relationships can be linearized logarithmically, namely

$$y = a - bx$$

where: $y = \ln Me$ or $\ln Ep$ and $\ln Er$ \hfill (5)

$$a = \ln A$$

$$b = B$$

A and B are parameters, having different values for Me, Ep and Er. From equation (5) we get the following three formulas:

I. Forest coverage ratio versus annual sediment transportation module:

$$Me = A_1 e^{-B_1 x} \tag{6}$$

II. Forest coverage ratio versus soil erosion module per unit precipitation:

$$Ep = A_2 e^{-B_2 x} \tag{7}$$

III. Forest coverage ratio versus soil erosion module per unit runoff:

$$Er = A_3 e^{-B_3 x} \tag{8}$$

The parameters of A_1, B_1, A_2, B_2, A_3, B_3 are affected by such geomorphological features on the Loess Plateau as *mao* and *liang*. These parameters were determined for major geomorphological regions and are shown in Table 3.

TABLE 3

Values of A and B in Equations (6), (7), (8).

Value	Geomorphological features		
	Mao	Mao with liang	Rocky mountain with thin loess layers
A_1	15,000	8,800	4,080
B_1	0.0329	0.0331	0.033
A_2	36	23.3	8
B_2	0.0376	0.0385	0.0383
A_3	620	320	80
B_3	0.0313	0.0313	0.0642

Based on the same data of investigation, a curve of effectiveness of forest on sediment reduction was plotted in Figure 2, which shows that the effectiveness is particularly noticeable at low forest coverage ratios. The effectiveness is fairly good when x = 30 percent, in which case the effectiveness of forest on sediment reduction is about 60 percent. Based upon these results, it is possible to predict future potential sediment reduction by afforestation in the Loess Plateau of the middle reaches of the Yellow River.

In addition, the effect of forest on the dilution of the silt content in river water is basically not affected by the sizes of river basins. At the same time we have found that the reduction rate of sediment charge affected by forest cover is several times more than the

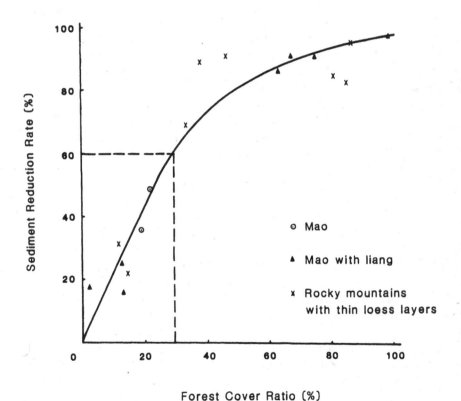

Figure 2. Effectiveness of forest on sediment reduction

reduction rate of water discharge; that the forest can delay the flood period by 2–6 times; and that the occurrence time of peak discharge can be delayed by 5–10 times. These futures of sediment charge and flood discharge could be favorable for sediment transportation in the downstream channel of the Yellow River. In a word, the forest cover in the Loess Plateau can effectively decrease a large quantity of sediment but only a relatively small amount of water discharge in the flood recession period.

A large forest cover can also bring about other positive effects on the environment. We have noted that the precipitation in the forested regions of the Loess Plateau is about 25–75 mm (1–3 in) more than that of the unforested regions. Owing to the effect of increased humidity and decreased temperature caused by the forest in wet years and during flood seasons, the amount of evapotranspiration inside a forest and under the trees also has decreased. The forest cover intercepts approximately 12–30 percent of the total annual precipitation or about 100 mm. This part of the precipitation lost by interception contributes to additional evaporation in the forested regions and increases the humidity of the air. The growth of a forest leads to a higher percolation capacity on the ground surface. So, a large amount of rainfall and surface water infiltrates underground to recharge the groundwater. While flood water is diminished, the groundwater is increased. In such a case, the compensation effect in the forested regions of the Loess Plateau is formed. Because of the regulating function of the forest, the proportion of groundwater runoff can account for 85 percent of the total annual runoff, but in unforested regions underground runoff makes up only 30–40 percent of the total. Thus underground runoff in forest regions is 2–3 times greater than that of unforested regions. If the interflow that occurs in every flood is added, the amount of underground water in forested regions will make up approximately 95 percent of the total annual runoff. Thanks to this compensation effect, the water regime of a river in a forested region of the Loess Plateau can become stable, thus reducing the hazards of waterlogging and drought in the forested region.

In a word, forest can play a positive and comprehensive role in the control of soil erosion and in regulating water regimes. Therefore, in planning the harnessing of the Yellow River, afforestation and reforestation as well as comprehensive soil conservation measures should be taken as fundamental approaches.

Vast areas of the Loess Plateau have favorable conditions for afforestation. Based on the data on humidity, temperature and soil property, which we obtained, we have estimated that in the loess hills region alone, where soil erosion is the most severe, the total area suitable for reforestation may amount to 4,000,000 ha, including the severely eroded watersheds of the Yanhe, the middle and lower reaches of the Qingjianhe, the lower reaches of the Wudinghe as well as the regions south of the Sanchuanhe (Figure 1). As for the areas north of these regions, where the climate is more arid, afforestation is also possible but more human efforts are required.

CONCLUSION

It is clear from this study that afforestation and reforestation can have a strong and positive effect on the control of soil erosion on the Loess Plateau. It can also improve the region's microclimatic conditions, regulate water regimes, and prevent flooding and drought. In addition, the Loess Plateau was a widely forested area in historical times, and at present it still has fairly good natural conditions for reforestation. We believe that in harnessing the Yellow River and in developing the economy of the Loess Plateau region, reforestation is not only feasible but also necessary. What remains to be studied are the locations and scales of reforestation.

NOTE

1. We wish to thank Professor Laurence J.C. Ma, Department of Geography, The University of Akron, for his comments on this paper. Mr. Liang Jianming participated in the research.

LITERATURE CITED

Editorial Committee on "China's Physical Geography," Academia Sinica, 1981, *China's Physical Geography: Surface Water*. Beijing: Sciences Press.

Gong, Shiyang and Deqi Jiang, 1979, Soil erosion and its control in small watersheds of the Loess Plateau. *Scientia Sinica*, Vol. 22, No. 11, 1,302–1,313.

Hewlett, John D., 1981, *Principles of Forest Hydrology*. Athens, Ga.: University of Georgia Press.

Liu, Changming, 1981, The influence of forest cover upon annual runoff in the Loess Plateau of China. In Laurence J.C. Ma and Allen G. Noble, editors, *The Environment: Chinese and American Views*. New York: Methuen and Co., pp. 131-142.

Assessment of Potential Agricultural Land in Western China with a Geographic Information System (GIS)

R. Welch, Y.R. Hsu, and C.W. Pannell

In 1981 China had approximately 10 percent of its total land area of 9.6 million sq km available for crop cultivation (*Beijing Review*, 1981). However, the cultivated land area has declined slightly in recent years due to urban expansion, and efforts has been directed at locating new lands suitable for agricultural production (Welch, Lo and Pannell, 1979; *Beijing Review*, 1984). The objective of this paper is to illustrate the use of a geographic information system (GIS) for this purpose. The GIS approach involves the construction of a computer data base in which layers of information, registered to a map reference system, are stored and may be recalled to model or evaluate potential land development (Fig. 1).

Most investigations of the GIS approach have been undertaken in the United States with the conclusion that it is an efficient tool for resource management and planning (Anderson, Guptill, Hallam and Mitchell, 1977; Tomlin and Berry, 1979; and Man and Breese, 1981). However, these studies were conducted in an environment where collateral data were readily available and field checks easily conducted. In remote areas such as western China, the possibilities for establishing a GIS data base are limited by the availability of statistical and map information. Therefore, important goals here are to demonstrate the possibilities for developing a data base from Landsat image data, available maps, and limited collateral information, and for using this data base to produce a provisional assessment of the potential for new agricultural lands in the Xinjiang Autonomous Region (A.R.).

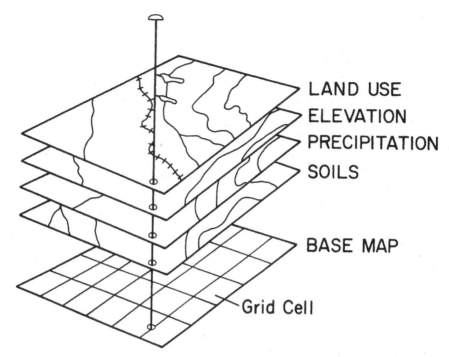

Figure 1. Schematic diagram of a geographic information system (GIS). In a GIS, layers of information registered to a map base are stored in a computer memory for analysis through special algorithms.

THE XINJIANG AUTONOMOUS REGION STUDY AREA

The Xinjiang, A.R. (1,600,000 sq km), located in China's far west, is an arid land of mountains, desert basins, grasslands, and irrigated farmlands in which the physical environment plays an important role in controlling human activities. Urban centers such as Urumqi (estimated 1980 population 800,000) are located along major transportation lines near available water. Where environmental conditions permit, use of the land is primarily for agricultural purposes (McMillen, 1979). Precipitation, soil type, elevation, and slope are major variables influencing land use.

The area selected for this study occupies 2652 sq km centered on the city of Urumqi (Figs. 2 and 3). Urumqi lies in a corridor linking the Junggar Basin northwest of the city to the Turpan Depression and Tarim Basin located to the south and east (Figs. 3 and 4). The

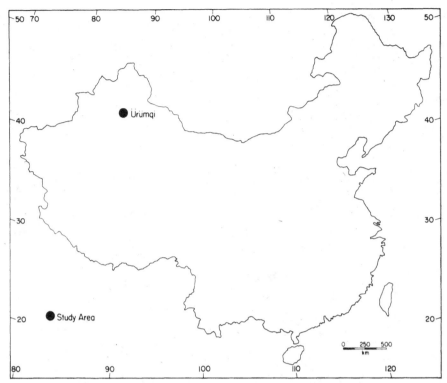

Figure 2. Location map of study area. The city of Urumqi, Xinjiang Autonomous Region, is the focal point of the study area.

city is an important administrative, transportation, agricultural, and industrial center which depends on the resources and agricultural activities of the region (CIA, 1971; McMillen, 1979).

Segments of the Tian Shan and related other ranges (the Bogda Feng) with elevations to 5400 m are located to the south and east of the study area. These highlands form an approximately east-west oriented ecological divide. During the months of April through September, winds are predominantly from the northwest and bring moisture to the north slopes of the mountains. For example, annual precipitation at Urumqi on the north slope averages about 267 mm/year with a pronounced summer maximum of about 25-35 mm/month.

So modest is the precipitation in the study area that almost all row cropping depends on irrigation. Precipitation at the higher elevations (200 m) is more than double that at Urumqi (elevation

Figure 3. Landsat image of study area. Arrow in center depicts location of Urumqi. Landsat MSS, Band 7, ERTS E-7232-04113-7 of 11 September 1975.

760 m), whereas approximately 200 km southeast of Urumqi in the rain shadow of the Bogda range, the Turpan Depression has an average precipitation of only 25 mm/year. Other important physical characteristics of the study area include variations in local relief that range from comparatively low areas in the plain around Urumqi to the steep slopes of the Bogda range at elevations above 3000 m.

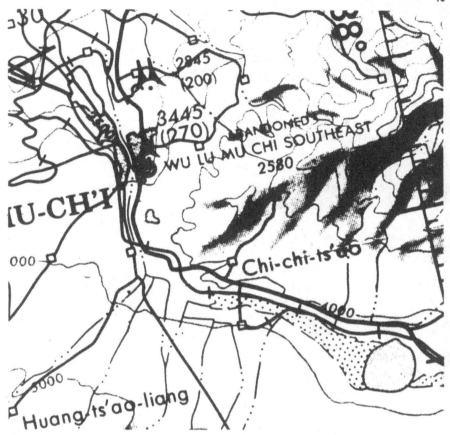

Figure 4. Photographic enlargement of Operational Navigation Chart (ONC F-7) Defense Mapping Agency (1975) for the study area.

According to a survey conducted in the 1950s by the Chinese Academy of Sciences, Xinjiang has some 16.5 million hectares of marginal land with soil sufficiently fertile to support agriculture. Since 1956, the Chinese Academy of Sciences has sent groups of scientists to Xinjiang to investigate the possibility of developing these marginal lands for agricultural uses.

The availability of water is a major problem throughout Xinjiang (Institute of Geography, 1960). State farms and communes have emphasized water conservancy and constructed a large number of new drainage channels, aqueducts, and wells to insure a reliable supply of water. For example, improvements in water conservancy and mechanization doubled Xinjiang's cultivated land from 1,221,860 ha in 1949 to 2,440,485 ha in 1964 (Kuo, 1976). By the end of 1963, the Xinjiang Production Construction Corps, a land

44

reclamation organization, had established more than 140 mechanized state farms and had reclaimed some 740,890 ha of marginal lands (Sai, 1959; New China News Agency, 1964).

DATA BASE DEVELOPMENT

In order to assess land potential in the Urumqi area, data on land use/cover, elevation, precipitation, slope, soils, surface water, and transportation were required. In addition, a topographic map base to which the various data sets could be registered was essential to the study. The only topographic map (Fig. 4) of this remote region available to the investigators was an Operational Navigation Chart (ONC F-7) of 1:1,000,000 scale with 500 and 1000 foot contour intervals (DMA, 1975). This map was photographically enlarged to 1:250,000 scale and served as the base to which all data sets were registered. The methods for generating the various data sets are discussed in the following section.

Land Use/Cover (Fig. 5)

Attempts to classify land use/cover by digital analyses of a Landsat multispectral scanner (MSS) computer compatible tape (CCT) of the area were frustrated by the rugged terrain which caused deep shadows that obscured large portions of the study area. Thus, the boundaries of the 10 land use/cover classes in Figure 5 were derived from visual analysis of false color composite Landsat images and transferred to the 1:250,000 scale enlargement of ONC F-7.

In order to develop coded information on land use/cover, a grid with a 1000 x 1000 m (4 x 4 mm) cell size corresponding to 100 ha was registered to the map using well-defined control points to insure correct alignment. Each of the 2652 grid cells for the study area was assigned a code number from 1 to 10 representing one of the land use classes. Thus, each grid cell was referenced by an X (column) and Y (row) coordinate, and assigned a Z value corresponding to the appropriate land use/cover class. This data set constituted a *layer* of land use/cover information and was stored as a computer disk file.

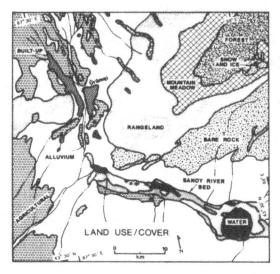

Figure 5. Land use/cover as determined from the interpretation of the Landsat image and from scientific surveys, Murzayev and Chou (1959), and Institute of Geography (1960).

Elevation (Fig. 6)

Elevations relate to land use/cover and precipitation, and values in meters were required for each grid cell. These elevation data were also needed for the computation of slopes.

The 1000 x 1000 m (4 x 4 mm) grid was registered to the 1:250,000 scale enlargement of ONC F-7 and the contour lines transferred from the map to the grid. From these contour lines (1000 foot interval), spot elevations to the nearest 200 feet were interpolated for each grid cell. These values were subsequently converted to meters and coded to provide a *layer* of elevation data.

Elevation, which reflects variations in the amount of precipitation as well as temperature, also may be used to differentiate vegetation as shown in Figure 5. At elevations to 1000 m, desert shrubs and semishrubs with some grasses prevail; trees are found along water courses. Above 1000 m, a steppe-like cover (rangeland) becomes prominent and extends to approximately 1600 m. As elevations increase above 1600 m, rangeland grades into a meadow and spruce forest belt which extends to about 2800 m. Above the treeline, at approximately 3300 m, snow and ice are encountered.

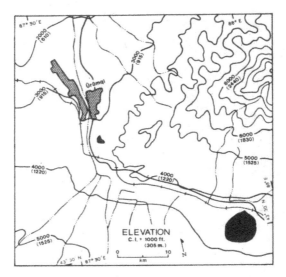

Figure 6. Contour map of the study area based on navigation chart, ONC F-7 (1975).

Slope

Slope, which affects the depth of soil, water runoff, and rate of erosion, influences human activities, particularly in the mountain areas. A slope value for each grid cell was calculated based on the difference in elevation between a given grid cell and the highest and lowest elevations of the surrounding cells. These values provide a layer of slope information.

Precipitation (Fig. 7)

In an arid region such as this, the amount of precipitation and its spatial distribution are critical to agricultural, pastoral, and forestry practices. Consequently, a representative layer of precipitation data for the summer growing season was required. Unfortunately, few weather stations are located in this portion of China, so only limited data were available. Five stations in the vicinity of the study area were plotted at their appropriate locations, and an interpolation of August (annual maximum) precipitation values was undertaken to determine the spatial distribution and amounts of summer rainfall. Each 1000 x 1000 m grid cell as then assigned a precipitation value for the month of August.

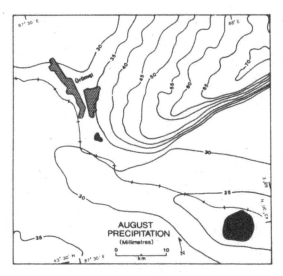

Figure 7. August precipitation as determined from interpolations of data on five neighboring stations. *Atlas of Chinese Climatology* (1960).

Soils (Fig. 8)

Soils in this region are broadly classified as aridisols, mollisols, or spodosols according to the Seventh Approximation Classification (U.S. Department of Agriculture, 1960). Traditional descriptive terms from the older Marbut classification have been used for this study because of their familiarity. The main types are the alkaline, desert and alluvial soils, the richer chestnut and brown earths, and the chemically neutral forest and meadow soils found in the mountains. Most agricultural development in this study area has taken place on the desert or chestnut and brown soils. The seven broad soil types delimited in Figure 8 are based on available data for precipitation, elevation, slope, vegetation, and on descriptions taken from Chinese scientific surveys (Murzayev and Chou, 1959; and Institute of Geography, 1960). The boundaries for the different soil types were derived by correlating the Landsat images with available maps and descriptive soil surveys of the region (Ren, Yang and Bao, 1979). Soil-type boundaries were transferred to the enlarged base map, and a layer of soils information was produced by coding each of the 1000 x 1000 m grid cells.

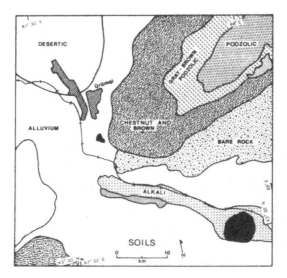

Figure 8. Soils map based on descriptive and scientific surveys, Murzayev and Chou (1959), Institute of Geography (1960), and Ren, Bao and Cheng (1979), as well as interpretation of Landsat image data.

Surface Water

Surface streams, largely derived from melting snows and glaciers, are an important source of irrigation water in the study area. Although characterized by marked variation in rate of discharge, streams are full during the warm growing season and provide irrigation water for summer season agriculture and the expansion of farmlands in arid areas. Consequently, the number of streams located in each grid cell was coded to create a data layer for surface water.

Transportation

Transportation routes are an important factor in the development of a remote area. They can facilitate the movement of equipment, fertilizer, labor, and other inputs to the developing area and can be used to ship grains, vegetables, and other commodities to market. To build transportation systems in a remote area is expensive. Thus, lands close to the existing transportation network are more accessible and a logical choice for agricultural development.

Major and secondary highways as well as railroads were delineated by registering the 1000 x 1000 m grid to the base map and transferring the transportation net from the map to the grid. Each grid cell was then assigned a code number according to the proximity of major and secondary highways and/or the railroad to create a layer of transportation information.

USE OF THE GIS TO DETERMINE POTENTIAL AGRICULTURAL LAND

The layers of information were stored on IBM 370/158 computer disk files and manipulated with the aid of GIS software routines. In this instance the CONversational GRID (CONGRID) program was employed to determine and map the spatial distribution of potential agricultural land in the Urumqi area. CONGRID is based on set theory and uses intersection, union, and linear combination algorithms to isolate grid cells satisfying predefined conditions for land use/cover, elevation, slope, precipitation, soils, etc. (Hokans, 1979).

For the arid Urumqi area, the land which currently supports agriculture is located on the relatively flat areas at elevations of less than 1000 m which have desert or chestnut brown soils, and August precipitation values of greater than 25 mm. Geographic principles dictate that land along streams which is adjacent to transportation routes also has potential for agricultural development. On the other hand, the infertile soils, steep slopes, and climatic factors limit the possibilities for agricultural activities at elevations above 2000 m.

Guided by these considerations, an initial effort was made to identify and map all grid cells meeting the following conditions for potential agricultural land (Fig. 9):

1. Slopes of less than 5 percent and 20 percent.
2. Desert or chestnut and brown soils.
3. August precipitation values in 5 intervals from 25 to more than 60 mm.

In Figure 9 the grid cells meeting the established criteria are coded according to precipitation values. A total area of 70,000 ha of potential agricultural land is indicated for slopes of less than 5 percent. If this map is compared to Figure 5 in which 36,400 ha of agricultural land have been delineated, it is evident that the

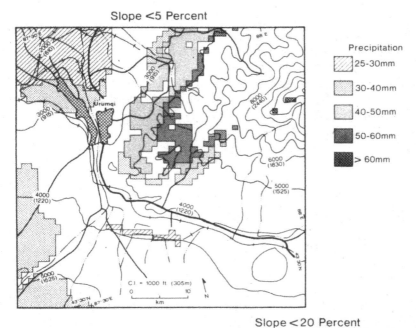
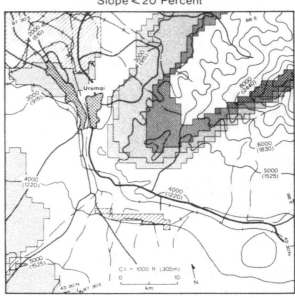

Figure 9. Maps of potential agricultural land produced with the GIS and based on slopes of less than 5 to 20 percent, desert or chestnut and brown soils and August precipitation values.

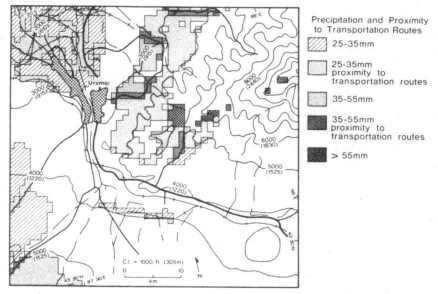

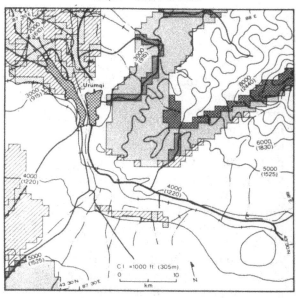

Figure 10. Map of potential agricultural land produced with the GIS and based on slopes of less than 5 to 20 percent in combination with desert or chestnut brown soils, August precipitation values from 25 to more than 55 mm, and proximity to transportation routes.

52

majority of the potential new agricultural land corresponds to the rangeland east of Urumqi. If slopes to 20 percent are considered acceptable, an additional 8,500 ha of potential agricultural land is available.

In Figure 10, cells have been ranked according to suitability for agricultural activities based on weighted combinations of soils, precipitation, and proximity to transportation routes. Although a total of over 60,000 ha of potential agricultural land are mapped, only 3400 and 4300 ha of land for the 5 and 20 percent slope conditions respectively have the favorable combination of good soil, August precipitation in excess of 35 mm, and proximity to transportation routes. Again, the area immediately east of Urumqi appears best suited for agricultural development.

From the above analyses it is clear that the use of the GIS approach does permit the delineation of potential agricultural land in this remote area of China according to defined attributes. However, more detailed input from local sources is required to verify provisional conclusions based on the GIS approach.

CONCLUSION

This GIS approach, which permits variables to be stored in a computer memory as layers of information registered to a map base, provides a powerful mechanism for delineating potential agricultural lands. In this study, a data base was created from Landsat images, available maps, and interpolation techniques to include information on land use/cover, elevation, transportation networks, streamflows, slope, precipitation, and soils. By employing the GIS software, approximately 30,000 to 40,000 ha of potential new agricultural lands were identified in the 265,200 ha study area. The most productive land is relatively flat and is characterized by desert or chestnut and brown soils; precipitation in excess of 25 mm for August; and proximity to streams and transportation routes.

This demonstration project indicates the possibility for evaluating potential new agricultural lands in developing countries with a GIS. As the resolution of remotely sensed data is improved and more detailed information is made available, the GIS approach should prove to be a powerful tool for the management of the resources of remote areas.

LITERATURE CITED

Anderson, K. E., S. C. Guptill, C. Hallam and W. B. Mitchell, 1977, Developing and using a Geographic Information System for handling and analyzing land resource data, *Remote Sensing of the Electro-Magnetic Spectrum*, Vol. 4, No. 4, pp. 67–83.

Beijing Review, 1981, Composition of China's land resources, Vol. 24, No. 37, p. 27.

Beijing Review, 1984, China surveys land resources, Vol. 27, No. 3, p. 10.

Central Intelligence Agency (CIA), 1971, *People's Republic of China Atlas*, Washington, D.C.: U.S. Government Printing Office.

Defense Mapping Agency (DMA), 1975, Operational Navigation Chart, (ONC F-7, Mongolia, People's Republic of China, USSR, 1:1,000,000).

Hokans, Richard H., 1979, *Georgia Georeference Resource Information Timesharing System*, Multifunctional Forest Planning Research Group, School of Forest Resources, University of Georgia, Report #3, August, pp. 64–75.

Institute of Geography, Academy of Sciences, USSR and Sinkiang Complex Expedition, Academy of Sciences, People's Republic of China, 1960, *Soviet-Chinese Study of the Geography of Sinkiang* (JPRS: 15,084 of 31 August 1962), Washington, D.C.: Joint Publications Research Service.

Kuo, Leslie T. C., 1976, *Agriculture in the People's Republic of China*, New York: Praeger Publishers.

Man, K. D. and J. A. Breese, 1981, Forest management application of Landsat data in a Geographic Information System, *Proceedings* of Pecora VII Symposium, pp. 330–340.

McMillen, Donald H., 1979, *Chinese Communist Power and Policy in Xinjiang*, Boulder, Colorado: Westview Press.

Murzayev, E. M. and Chou, Li-san, 1959, *Natural Conditions in the Sinkiang Uighur Autonomous Region* (JPRS: 18,689 of 15 April 1963), Washington, D.C.: Joint Publications Research Service.

New China News Agency, 1964, Urumchi, November 13 as cited in Kuo, 1976.

Ren, Meie, Yang Renzhang, and Bao Haosheng, 1979, *Zongguo dzran dili gangyao* (An Outline of China's Physical Geography), Beijing: Commercial Press (in Chinese).

Sai Tu-ting, Ten years of great achievements in Sinkiang's agriculture, *Zhongguo Nongbao*, No. 19, 1959, pp. 19–23 (as cited in Kuo, 1976).

Tomlin, C. D. and J. K. Berry, 1979, A mathematical structure for cartographic modeling in environmental analysis, 39th Symposium *Proceedings* of the American Congress on Surveying and Mapping, pp. 209–284.

U.S. Department of Agriculture, Soil Conservation Service, Soil Survey Staff, 1960, *Soil Classification, A Comprehensive Seventh Approximation*, Washington, D.C.: U.S. Government Printing Office.

Welch, R., H. C. Lo and C. W. Pannell, Mapping China's new agricultural lands, *Photogrammetric Engineering and Remote Sensing*, Vol. 45, No. 9, 1979, pp. 1211–1288.

The Changing Rural Landscape of China: A Study of Gaohe Xian, Guangdong

T.N. Chiu
C.K. Leung

INTRODUCTION

The reformist approach of Chinese planners dominates economic policymaking in Peking today. Although the main system remains highly regulated, a gradual decentralization of investment decision-making has been characteristic of the "readjustments" launched by the leadership since the late 1970s (Xue, 1981; *Beijing Review*, Feb. 4, 1980; Hua, 1979). New economic theory recognizes the principle of material interests and allows market forces to play some part in determining the production of goods and services. Among the more significant reforms in the system of economic management are the delegation of more independence to enterprises at the grass roots levels and to local authorities to make their own decisions; the restoration of a commercial network not entirely subject to the state market system; and the granting of extraordinary commercial autonomy to some provinces.

Since 1978 changes in rural policy have encouraged the drive toward a diversified economy which has replaced the former singular emphasis on food grain production. The specialization and division of labor, which are intended to make the best use of indigenous resources and the environment, including traditional skills and locational advantages relative to input and market sources, are to be instated as part of a long-term policy at the expense of "absolute equalitarianism" (*Beijing Review*, Nov. 10, 1980; Jan. 19, 1981; Mar. 16, 1981). The experimental nature of the new policies has been recognized and modifications, especially in the management of production, are expected to be an ongoing necessity.

One of the locational advantages enjoyed by the rural communes in the coastal provinces of China is the proximity to large urban markets and to export facilities provided by the transportation centers. Relieved from ties of the grain-oriented production policy, rural communes have been urged to develop cash crop production with a view to establishing themselves as export bases (*Hongqi*, 1980). But the government cautions that liberalization of control of export oriented agriculture should not lead to an undisciplined reduction in the acreage for food crops. The majority of the rural population will continue to rely on its own food supply (*Hongqi*, 1981). Striking a balance between food production (to retain a degree of self-sufficiency) and economic crop production (to satisfy urban markets and export demands) will require a close scrutiny of the resources and the trends of product changes by decision-makers at the grass roots level. Important changes and readjustments for those rural communes with a strong export potential are under way.

The changing rural landscape is exemplified by the following account of the evolution of agricultural production in Gaohe, a county (xian) southwest of Guangzhou, the capital of Guangdong province. This report presents part of the findings of one of those rare occasions when organized data collected by a team of university students from Hong Kong were available. Field data were augmented by information gathered both before and after the team's visit, through the authors' discussions with people in charge of production and administration at different levels. The field investigation, which included field mapping and interviews using a questionnaire, was assisted by a team of teachers from the county high school. Their presence among the survey groups and the common dialect spoken by the interviewers and the interviewees offered much help in easing suspicions about the purpose and intention of the survey and in securing more reliable results from the respondents, the majority of whom had never been approached by an interviewer.

Obvious gaps in the information obtained can be seen. There is limited access to official records, and there are incomplete answers to inquiries, but this study reveals the extent to which data, especially statistical data related to agricultural production at the xian level, might be compiled and made ready to guide official strategy in the coming period of important decision-making. Unless otherwise stated, all figures given in this report are derived from field data or from unpublished administrative reports of the xian government.

INTRODUCTION TO THE GEOGRAPHY OF GAOHE

With a total area of about 2,100 km^2, Gaohe xian lies 30 km southwest of Guangzhou and 70 km northwest of Macau (Figure 1). It originated from the merging together, administratively in 1958, of the two separate xian of Gaoming and Heshan, and derived its name from the first Chinese characters of these two xian. In the period 1958–1981, Gaohe was one of the 94 xian of Guangdong province and was administered under the Foshan District, one of the 7 districts (diqu) of the province (Figure 2).[1] Topographically, it is dominated in the center by Juhmu Shan, the easternmost part of the much more mountainous Yunwu Shan that forms the backbone of Guangdong west of Xi Jiang. Juhmu Shan (Figure 3), rising 813 m from the deltaic plain of the Xi Jiang, effectively divides Gaohe into two parts. The western part consists of several basins enclosed by the extensions of ranges and foothills from Juhmu Shan toward the main body of Yunwu Shan. The larger part of these basins, each occupied by a commune, drains north and east into the Cang Jiang, a tributary to the Xi Jiang in its deltaic section. The eastern slopes of Juhmu Shan, relatively steeper and less interrupted, meet the flood plains of the Xi Jiang rather abruptly with little foothill area. Apart from isolated hills and mounds, eastern Gaohe is a vast plain made up of deposits both from the Xi Jiang flood waters and from denudation by the streams draining from Juhmu Shan.

In traditional Chinese geographic literature, the territory of Gaohe is considered an integral part of the central subregion of Guangdong province (Figure 4) (Liang, 1956; Xu, 1957; Sun, 1959; Chen, 1978). There are many studies dealing with one specific district in this subregion, namely, the Pearl River Delta. The areas outside the delta, including Gaohe, have received only occasional mention, and this literature concerns only the more significant concentrations of settlement such as Zhaoqing, Jiangmen, or Taishan. Although

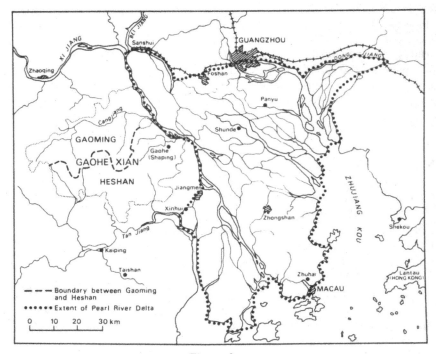

Figure 1

bordering on the Xi Jiang river on its eastern side, Gaohe lies clearly outside the delta area and contains no large cities (Zhong and Wang, 1958) (Figure 1). Shaping, the seat of the xian government, is only a small rural market and ranks very low in the hierarchy of central places in the subregion (Chan, 1977). The literature reflects the dominance of the South China economy by the productive delta area, which, in turn, is dominated by the urban centers of Guangzhou, Foshan, Zhongshan, Shunde, and Jiangmen. Shaping appears dwarfed by its proximity to several high-order centers. The territory of Gaohe xian is rendered a largely agricultural role to provide much needed primary produce. The xian exemplifies a relatively unobtrusive rural area that lies in close proximity to several developed centers, including Macau and Hong Kong, and with the more recently developed and nearby Zhuhai and Shenzhen Special Economic Zones (SEZs). Gaohe is near enough to Hong Kong, for example, for its rural families to be bombarded by the daily television programs from this extremely capitalistic and *laissez-faire* economy. The Gaohe residents have also watched, from across the Xi Jiang, the enlivening of the rural economy in other Pearl River Delta xian, such as Shunde and Zhongshan. These areas enjoy better potential for food production and export, advantages derived from their site and situation on the largest alluvial plain of South China and from the fact that they are a part of a direct catchment area supplying the almost insatiable markets of Hong Kong, Macau, Guangzhou, and the growing SEZs. Perceived from the more isolated location of Gaohe, the growth generated by the new economic interactions as a result of the liberalization of government policies and the dynamism of the SEZs seems to be shrouded by the distance from the Pearl River Estuary (Figure 1).

Encouraged by the central government's new policy, the xian authority feels a strong urge to upgrade the xian economy by restructuring its agriculture and by developing industry. While its geographic location relative to other agricultural areas and markets is accepted as a natural disadvantage, it is trying to exploit its locational advantage at the crossroads made by the arterial highway

Figure 2

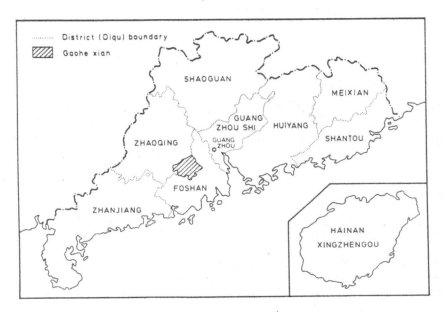

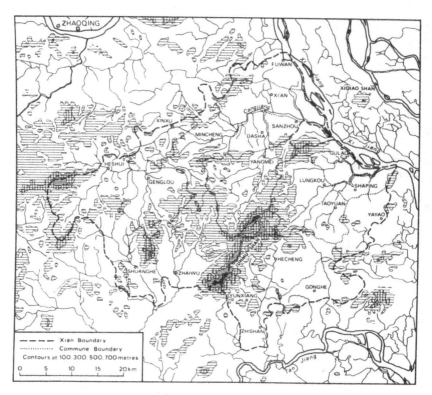

Figure 3

linking Guangzhou and Zhanjiang, the rapidly growing deep sea port of South China and designated base for offshore oil prospecting, and the highway that joins Jiangmen, the largest port on the Pearl River Delta, and Zhaoqing, the port on the Xi Jiang immediately above the delta section (Figure 1).

AGRICULTURAL DEVELOPMENT

The agricultural economy of the entire central Guangdong subregion shares the characteristics of its type area, the delta, to varying extents. Modifications in the scale and type of production are made necessary by the difficult relief outside the alluvial plain. Instead of the combined paddy-sugarcane-mulberry and pisciculture system, which is typical of the deltaic lowlands, the hilly districts to the west and the north of the Pearl River Delta are more important for their paddy rice and subsidiary food crops such as sweet potatoes, wheat, and vegetables (Zhong, 1980). Only about 20-40 percent of the lowland in Gaohe and 10-20 percent of its land above 30 meters are under cultivation as compared with an average of over 50 percent in the delta area (Liang, 1956). Gaoming, the northern half of Gaohe, was one of the more important rice producing districts outside the delta area. Its surplus rice output used to be shipped to Guangzhou, but it was the fish fry supply from the streams of the district that constituted its most important contribution to the agricultural economy of the delta area. On the other hand, Heshan, the southern half of Gaohe, was more important for its tea and tobacco growing on hilly land. At one time the area planted with tea

Figure 4

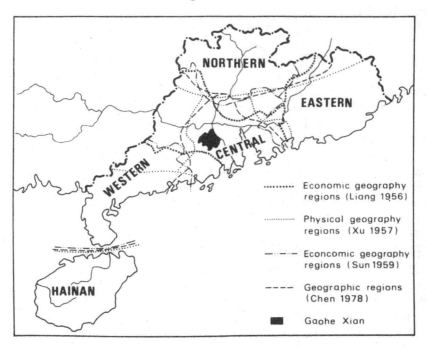

in Heshan accounted for half that in the province (Liang, 1956). Unlike Gaoming, Heshan had always been a food deficient area, producing only about one-third of its own need. Before 1949 food produced was estimated to be below 600 jin per capita in an average year (1 metric ton = 20 tan = 2,000 jin).

Changes in the agricultural scene came with the Communist regime. Within the first decade Gaohe went through the processes of land reform, cooperative, and communization movements. The redistribution of land ownership during the land reform, lasting from October 1950 to March 1953, is shown in Table 1. Attention is drawn particularly to the reversal in the share of land ownership by the two broad groups of poor and middle-class farmers and hired laborers and landlords, rich farmers, and other landowners. While 17.83 percent of the people, constituting the richer group, owned 71.45 percent of the land before land reform, the situation was changed by 1953 when the laborers, poor and middle-class farmers, representing 82.17 percent of the people, owned 87.15 percent of the land. This land reform movement was accompanied by confiscation and appropriation of 24,933 houses, 6,789 draught animals, 65,603 farm implements, and 15,768 tons of grain for redistribution among the peasantry. Land reform was followed by the formation of mutual-aid teams. By early 1954, 36.4 percent of the households had joined; there were 35,346 households organized into 6,156 teams. Elementary cooperatives were introduced in late 1953, but the response was slow. There were, by early 1955, 257 and, by late 1956, 683 cooperatives consisting of 89.8 percent of the households. By the end of 1957 and on the eve of the Great Leap Forward, 98.4 percent of all households had joined the cooperatives. By annexing some of the smaller cooperatives, the xian had 612 higher cooperatives just before the onset of the communization movement which, starting in August 1958 with the Taoyuan commune south of Shaping, seat of the xian government, very quickly encompassed the whole xian. In 1981 there were in Gaohe 20 communes heading 261 production brigades with a total population of approximately 510,000 (Figure 3).

The earliest evident benefits of the cooperative and the communization movements were seen in the water control schemes made possible by the concerted effort at cooperation and by the breaking down of irrational boundary constraints. Water control was recognized as the prerequisite to increase the productivity of the land. Before 1949 only 20,000 mu (about 5 percent) of the farmland was provided with some form of water regulation, such as small reservoirs impounded by low dams. Most other fields depended on whatever amount of water could be obtained from the streams which often ran dry in the cool season. Fields bordering the lower reaches of streams, especially where they joined a major river such as Tan Jiang and Cang Jiang were often subject to flood despite extensive dyke construction work throughout history (Figure 3). Floods that destroyed over 100,000 mu of crops were recorded in 1915, 1944, and 1947, and the flooded fields continued to suffer long periods of low productivity after the water had subsided. The areas most seriously affected were the low-lying parts in the Sanzhou, Dasha, and Xi'an communes. Before communization most cooperative efforts were spent repairing and strengthening existing dykes.

Since 1958 specific projects to deal with problem areas were carried out, largely in the form of water storage in the source regions of streams and drainage in low-lying areas. Figure 5 shows the distribution and the capacities of these works to 1979. It may be noted that 70.9 percent (89.3 million m^3) of the storage capacity is found in the five communes sharing the mountainous core of Gaohe, while 73.3 percent (8,395 kilowatts) of the pumping capacity is found in the four communes sharing the lowland where the Cang Jiang joins the Xi Jiang. Sluice gates were constructed near the exit to the larger river in order to prevent the reverse flow of water up the Cang Jiang when the Xi Jiang is in flood. Similar sluice gates were built on the Shaping river to protect the xian capital from the Xi Jiang flood waters. A total of 816 electric pumping stations were installed in the low-lying areas to regulate the flow. By the end of 1979, 547,000 mu of the farmland in Gaohe, about 80 percent of the total, were effectively irrigated, and 134,700 mu were provided with drainage. Among these 547,000 mu, 406,700 mu were protected from drought or flood and could be counted on to give sustained yield.

During these construction processes, the opportunity was taken to improve the navigability of the main channels that provided much needed access to some market centers such as Shaping, Sanzhou, Mingcheng, and Gulao. Electric power generation is another development that came with water control. Juhmu Shan, the mountainous backbone of Gaohe, offered many favorable sites for such projects. There were 33 medium to small power plants where the energy of falling water was harnessed to supplement the power supply from the main provincial power grid. As Table 2 and Figure 5 would indicate, communes abutting Juhmu Shan led the xian in hydroelectric power generation. In addition, there were 180 points scattered all over the xian where small generators converted the

TABLE 1

Changes in Land Holding Resulting from Land Reform (1950-53)

Class	Persons		Households		Land ownership			
					Before Land Reform		After Land Reform	
	Number	%	Number	%	No. of Mu*	%	No. of Mu*	%
Hired laborers	26,952	8.42	8,211	8.45	3,430	0.56	44,845	6.6
Poor farmers	124,654	38.95	41,255	42.46	59,277	8.74	333,301	49.2
Middle farmers	111,372	34.8	28,472	29.3	130,521	19.25	212,614	31.35
Subtotal	262,978	82.17	77,948	80.2	193,228	28.55	590,760	87.15
Rich farmers	10,255	3.2	2,599	2.64	43,834	6.47	20,340	3.0
Landlord	17,727	5.53	4,212	4.34	416,917	61.48	35,271	5.2
Other landowners	29,113	9.1	12,407	12.78	24,009	3.5	31,617	4.65
Subtotal	57,095	17.83	19,218	19.76	484,760	71.45	87,228	12.85
Total	320,073	100	97,156	100	677,988	100	677,988	100

* 1 mu = 0.067 hectare = 0.164 acre

energy of short waterfalls to provide power for nearby farm work or for water pumps.

Change in the Crop System

With the water situation improved and with state pressure to produce more food, those districts, which once yielded one crop of rice a year and which comprised mostly paddy fields reclaimed from swampy ground, were converted to yield two crops. Some fields were made to produce three crops a year, such as two crops of rice with one crop of wheat or green manure. In the hilly districts the

Figure 5

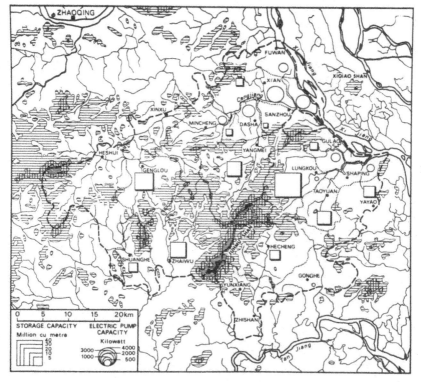

three crops were two crops of rice with tobacco or peanuts in winter. New strains of rice, particularly those with low stalks, which are resistant to lodging by strong wind, have been developed and propagated. Research into further seed improvement, especially aiming at pest control, continues. Other new inputs to raise crop production were chemical fertilizers. In 1979, for example, the total quantity of chemical fertilizers applied was 681,000 t, of which 55,000 t were nitrogenous compounds and 10,100 t were phosphates. Trials are being made with the use of new types of fertilizers testing the response of crops to additions of potassium and other trace elements.

TABLE 2

Distribution of Hydroelectricity Generation

Name of commune	Number of power plants	Capacity		Power generated 1979 (Thousand Kw)
		Generator	Kilowatt	
Yangmei	9	17	3090	5479
Mingcheng	2	4	575	1022
Zhaiwu	4	8	880	976
Hecheng	3	3	575	968
Lungkou	3	4	944	829
Heshui	3	6	538	840
Genglou	2	2	250	262
Gulao	1	3	525	904
Yunxiang	1	3	485	470
Taoyuan	1	1	125	393
Xi'an	1	1	40	37
Shuanghe	1	1	84	22
Gonghe	1	1	40	20
Xinxu	1	1	40	23
Total	32	54	8191	12245

Figure 6 is constructed from selected series of statistics which cover the post-liberation period and which reveal some important features of agricultural development in Gaohe. The total area sown in food crops increased rapidly following the Communist takeover and the land reform which made peasants the owners of the reward from their own land. It increased by 30 percent in five years to reach the peak of 1.29 million mu in 1954, a peak which has never been regained since. From 1955, the year in which the peasants began to be preoccupied by the transition from cooperatives through collectives to communes, which ended family ownership of not only land but also many other means of agricultural production, the area sown to food crops shrank back to its original size. The years of the Great Leap Forward were in fact a period of sharp decline in agriculture, which was reflected also in a sharp reduction in the areas sown in rice, the xian's most important crop. The contrast in the effects of the land reform and of the collective/commune movement on agriculture is also demonstrated in the peasants' attitude toward field management and protecting what they had sown. This can be seen from the amount of land that was sown with seeds but not harvested, as indicated by the shaded area in Figure 6. Before the collectivization and communization of the rural economy, nearly all land sown was reaped. The situation deteriorated after 1954 when the sharp decrease in the area sown was more than matched by a deep plunge in the area reaped. The national movement to expand production of iron and steel even at the commune level during the Great Leap Forward must have played its part in taking away the labor that should have been deployed to field management. A significant part of the farm labor was also diverted to the construction of the seven water storage and irrigation projects which were completed between 1957 and 1958. Rehabilitation efforts following the Great Leap Forward were nullified by catastrophic weather in the lean years of 1960-1962, and the gap between the area sown and the area reaped widened. For 1961 and 1962 more than 10 percent of the area sown with rice was not reaped. Normal conditions returned in 1964, and the area sown increased steadily with very little loss in harvest. Learning from the experience of previous years, farmers concentrated rice cultivation in the ecologically more suitable areas, and its acreage stagnated after 1972. The high figure of total sown acreage regained since 1972 was largely accounted for by the planting of more cash crops such as vegetables, sweet potatoes, tobacco, and peanuts (Figure 7).

With improved inputs and regulated water supply to the fields,

Figure 6

the per-mu yield of rice had risen appreciably, and by 1966 it was double that of the early liberation period (lower part of Figure 6). This accounts for the much steeper rise in the production figures for rice than the rise in area sown. However, neither the area sown with rice nor the per-mu yield had held steady for very long periods. As experiments with new strains of rice and new inputs were still being carried out, the figures of production fluctuated especially after 1970.

The hilly relief of the greater part of Gaohe encouraged a more diversified cropping system than that in the low-lying deltaic area. Tobacco, peanuts, and tea have long been important crops, and the area planted with these crops has been recorded since 1949. The graphs in Figure 7 showing the acreage planted with tobacco and peanuts reveal a pattern similar to that for rice cultivation (Figure 6), especially the decline of 1959–1960 between two peak periods and the general rising trend after 1966. However, the peak periods for tobacco and peanuts tend to occur after the peaks for rice. The pattern suggests that when the weather and other agronomic

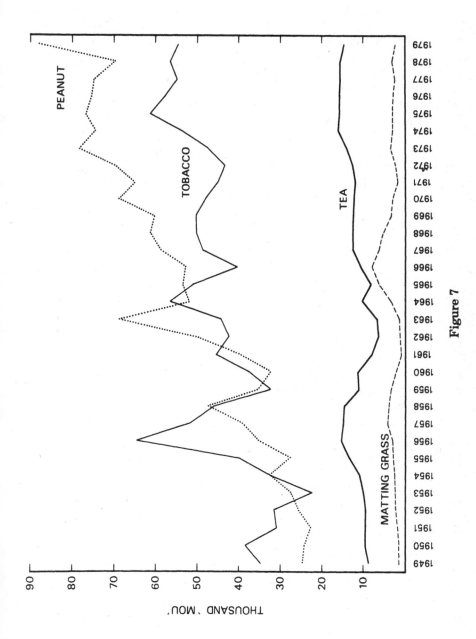

Figure 7

conditions were unfavorable for rice, production farmers would try to recoup some of the loss from growing cash crops. Gaohe is now the leading xian in Guangdong province for tobacco production, and export has been maintained above the 250 t figure over the past few years. The peanuts grown are for domestic oil supply, and the xian is self-sufficient in cooking oil.

Tea is produced also in the hilly areas. Unlike other cash crops, its production is in plantations or tea farms under central or state management. The earliest to be established was the tea farm at Zhaiwu on the southwestern side of Juhmu Shan. It was set up in 1949 at the District level.[2] It was followed in 1952 by a second plantation at Dasha, where the rolling topography was suitable for a combined system producing pond fish and paddy rice in addition to tea. These two plantations provide the bulk of the annual tea export of about 250 t. The area planted with tea increased moderately for a few years before 1974, but it has remained steady since then. Most attention has been given to improving the yield from existing areas through replanting and the use of sprinkler irrigation in the plantations.

Apart from the tea plantations, there are 13 other state farms in Gaohe (Table 3) with areas ranging from the 26,193 mu and 21,751 mu for forestry stations to the 160 mu for a fish fry nursery and 150 mu for a tea and livestock farm. Most of these farms specialize in one or two products such as paddy rice, fish, pine or fir trees, bamboo, and livestock with fruit. They also serve as research and extension stations for developing new strains and new breeds to supply the communes in Gaohe and in neighboring xian.

Gaohe has extensive areas of undulated land and mountain slopes. An estimated 1.7 million mu of such land could be put to best use by growing trees. At the time of the Communist takeover, only 0.1 million mu of forested land was left undestroyed by cutting or by hill fire. After 1949 tree planting lots were demarcated and put under government management at provincial levels. By 1979 there were in Gaohe 1.02 million mu of forested land, of which 0.7 million mu were planted with pine and 0.19 million mu were planted with fir. These are mainly for supplying much needed construction material and firewood in the villages (Table 4). The trees also provide the timber used in local small coal mines, and the saplings are used in an ambitious program of planting areas in major settlement points and along all inter-city highways. From 1974 onward, official encouragement has been given to intensifying the use of the mountain core of the xian for planting fir trees and to make Gaohe the key area in the Foshan administrative district for timber supply.

TABLE 3

State Farms in Gaohe

Location (commune)	Year of establishment	Management authority	Area mu	Number employed	Main items of production
Zhaiwu	1949	Foshan district	2,640	323	tea
Dasha	1952	Gaohe xian	1,819	348	tea
Gulao	1955	State fisheries bureau	16C	47	fish fry
Xi'an	1955	Foshan district	5,200	292	rice
Mingcheng	1958	State economic bureau	278	71	rice & fruit
Mingcheng	1958	Provincial	21,751	270	pine & fir timber
Taoyuan	1958	State livestock bureau	300	77	livestock & fruit
Zhisan	1958	Commune	n.a.*	94	bamboo
Lungkou	1958	Foshan district	26,193	225	pine & fir timber
Zhaiwu	1958	State commercial bureau	n.a.*	69	n.a.*
Mingcheng	1959	State agricultural bureau	440	183	rice
Genglou	1963	Commune	1,500	53	fruit
Yangmei	1973	State forestry bureau	1,470	102	timber
Shuanghe	1975	Provincial	12,287	5,521	rice
Mingcheng	1979	Gaohe xian	150	100	tea & livestock

*Data not available

71

TABLE 4

Forestry in Gaohe

	Area planted		Area cut*	
	mu total	of which mu in fir	mu total	timber in cubic meters
1975	51,583	29,520	6,459	10,507
1976	63,221	38,815	4,397	15,698
1977	71,381	31,392	4,941	9,916
1978	70,015	19,313	9,924	28,601
1979	36,707	10,231	8,663	14,129

*Trees cut are largely of pine and miscellaneous species. Timber includes firewood.

Livestock and Fishery

The number of livestock in Gaohe in 1949 is estimated at 36,900 head of cattle, 100,000 pigs, and 400,000 poultry. Important sideline activities of poultry and pig production have continued to aid in satisfying state purchase demands as well as the needs of individual pig and poultry producers. The number of pigs procured by the state has changed little in recent years, averaging in the late 1970s between 180,000 and 190,000 head annually for pigs and around half a million for poultry.[3] Cattle and buffalo have ceased to be an important source of meat. Because of the much needed power they can provide in the field and on the road, they could be sold for slaughtering only when certified as no longer useful to farm work. The number procured has continued to decrease from an annual average of 4,800 for the whole xian in the late 1950s to 1,200 in the late 1970s. Among the important livestock-breeding xian of Guangdong province, Gaohe has 6 livestock stations and 19 hatcheries under xian-level management with the task of developing and propagating improved breeds, including experimentation with animals introduced from foreign countries, not only for its own communes but also for other xian.

The main pond-fish-producing areas are Fuwan, Xi'an, Sanzhou, Gulao, and Shaping, all communes fronting the Xi Jiang or its confluences with major tributaries. In this low-lying land northeast of the mountain core, a dense network of ponds and channels are formed between both the natural and artificial Xi Jiang levees. This increases the number of swamps, which are converted to fish ponds. In 1949 the fish pond area was about 23,312 mu with an average output of 200 jin per mu. Besides the backward traditional breeding practice and management which accounted for the low yield at that time, fish production was dependent entirely on Jiujiang, a major fish pond district on the Pearl River Delta, for its supply of fish fry. By 1979 there were 38,986 mu of water surface, of which 22,539 mu were low-lying fish ponds; 12,480 mu were storage reservoirs and other water bodies impounded behind various retention structures; and 3,967 mu were natural surfaces such as drains, streams, and rivers. Pisciculture directly engages 13,200 farm laborers belonging to 205 production teams from 18 production brigades. They also have other agricultural work to attend to. For the year 1979 the total output of fish production is 80,972 tan, making an average yield of 333 jin per mu; this is in addition to the 2,700 tan caught from rivers and streams. Besides the fish fry farm set up at Gulao under state control (Table 3), the xian has four other smaller fish hatcheries run by communes, and together they produce about 200 million fry a year. About half of these go to the ponds and reservoirs of Gaohe for breeding; the other half supports pisciculture not only in the neighboring xian such as Gaoyao and Kaiping, but also as far away as Yangjiang, Yangchun, and Dianbai.

The output of fish for other years is shown in Figure 8, which also shows the quantities of state procurement from Gaohe xian of other livestock such as pigs, poultry, and cattle. Because of the difference in the unit of accounting for the different kinds of farm animals, the graphs in Figure 8 may not allow easy comparison. Several features related to the course of agricultural development can still be noted as common to all agricultural production. First, there was the initially gradual and then rapid production rise in the pre-communization days, followed by the sharp production decline in the Great Leap Forward. This pattern was observable not only in livestock but also in other agricultural production (Figures 6 and 7). Second, pisciculture, which is sensitive to adverse water and weather conditions, experienced greater decline than most other livestock production in the years 1961–62. The period between 1963

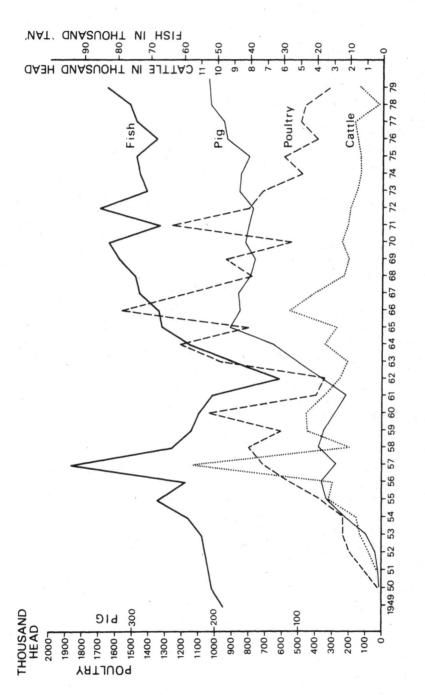

Figure 8

and 1969 is one of general recovery followed by a steady growth. But growth since 1970 seems to have been arrested, and varying trends are seen in the different lines of agricultural production during the latter half of the 1970s. The great fluctuations seen in the figures of poultry procurement confuse the picture. This could be explained by the fact that a large portion of poultry raising is very much a family pursuit even with communized agriculture, and hence may not be directly related to the overall health of the economy. Its continued decline in recent years may also be the result of reduced demand from state purchase which might have found alternative sources of supply elsewhere.

INDUSTRY AND TRANSPORTATION

Before 1949 urban growth and the development of industry and transport systems were concentrated in the Pearl River Delta—"the stronghold of imperialist influence" (Sun, 1959). In Gaohe the large factory type of manufacturing had been deterred by the lack of power sources and skilled labor. A negative effect must have been felt also from Gaohe's proximity to several urban centers that could provide much better support services to industry and greater accessibility to markets. The rich supply of agricultural products, however, had given rise to some processing industries such as silk reeling, spinning, food preserving, distilling, tobacco curing, and mat weaving. A small quantity of coal was obtained from Kaoming (Mingcheng commune) in a mine operated by manual labor, but the xian was far from self-sufficient in coal.

Since 1949 the scale of the traditional industries has been gradually enlarged, while new ones were added after the formation of communes. In Gaohe there are now nearly 500 small industrial enterprises and processing plants dealing with a great variety of farm products aiming at upgrading their value or transferability (*Nanfang ribao*, Sept. 14, 1981). The larger and more modern factories are located in the few market centers. Examples include electric fan making in Gulao, farm machinery in Hecheng, and wool spinning in Mingcheng. Shaping, the xian administrative center with a population of 18,374 (in 1980), has wool spinning, cement works, machine making, carriage assembling, and brewing. Since 1979 Shaping has embarked on a program of planned town renewal, which includes an attempt at attracting investment by preparing sites for an industrial district in the western sector. An important part of this urban development program is the improvement of the internal and the external transport system, especially the widening and straightening of streets in the old town center and the upgrading of the regional highway that skirts the city. This highway carried a daily traffic of 3,100 cars in 1980.

The road, which leads from Guangzhou to Zhanjiang and passes through Shaping, is only the southern one of two land routes reaching southwestern Guangdong from the provincial capital. The northern route, which passes through Sanshui, Zhaoqing, and Maoming, is actually shorter (395 km as compared with 470 km in the southern route). Although traditionally a larger volume of cargo and passengers was carried on the southern route, the road conditions were not suited to heavy vehicular traffic. The two lanes available to motorized transport are often obstructed by bicycles, animal-drawn carts, or tractor-drawn carriages. In the section between Foshan and Shaping, road transport is disrupted by two river crossings where car-ferries have to be used. Delays at these crossings have been found increasingly intolerable because the antiquated equipment and landing ramps are unable to cope with the daily crossing of more than 2,000 cars (*Nanfang ribao*, Oct. 2, 1981). The construction of bridges to replace these ferry crossings has been planned. Site investigation started in 1980.

Crossing this trunk road at Gaohe is another inter-regional highway that provides a road connection between Zhaoqing, the lowest river port on the Xi Jiang above the delta, and Jiangmen near the mouth of the Xi Jiang. This highway may be a very useful alternative access route when water conditions on the Xi Jiang are unfavorable for navigation (*Zhongguo Jiaotong Tuce*, 1979). These two trunk routes greatly enhanced the nodal position of Shaping and made Shaping one of the busiest markets for assembling and redistributing rural produce in the Foshan District. However, the convenience of access provided by the trunk roads and the waterway is concentrated on the eastern and the northern sides of the xian; roads joining the communes to the western side of Juhmu Shan are largely unsurfaced and of various standards of construction and maintenance.

CONCLUSION

The economy of Gaohe is still largely sustained by its agriculture. The xian enjoys a reputation for its production of tea, tobacco, and fish fry, in addition to other items common to the Pearl River Delta area. The land resources for further expansion in agriculture are limited, but attention has been turned toward achieving high yield with improved inputs. This has been facilitated by the recent changes in government policy which make it easier to introduce foreign breed stocks and methods and to enter into cooperative production projects and joint ventures with foreign institutions in agronomic research.[4] Improved stock is expected to increase pig and poultry production in the near future. Under the government directive to develop balanced agriculture and to make the best use of the local environment, the xian authority has earmarked Juhmu Shan as the key area for forestry development in which the planting of trees and the management of forest resources become the special task of 17 production brigades from the 6 communes sharing the mountain core.[5] Tea is another cash crop suited to the hilly land and the area planted is being expanded.

While the restrictions placed on traditional agriculture by the lack of level land are accepted as an obstacle, the wide range of topographic types offered by the mountains, basins, and foothills as well as flood plains within a short distance in the xian is an advantage because it offers a diversified environment suited to the new call to diversify agriculture. It is believed that Gaohe, situated between the established growth centers such as Guangzhou, Foshan, Shunde, and Jiangmen and the mountainous terrain south and west of Xi Jiang, can do much pioneering work in the search for a combination of agricultural enterprises suitable for emulation by the communes in the hilly areas of north and western Guangdong.

To help solve the mounting problem of employment for surplus farm labor, and to grasp the opportunity offered by the xian's proximity to the hearth of economic modernization since the inception of the special economic zones in Shenzhen and Zhuhai bordering Hong Kong and Macau, a start has been made to strengthen the industrial base by attracting foreign investment. Frequent contacts and negotiations with industrial entrepreneurs in Hong Kong and Macau were made between 1979 and 1981, and results are expected to begin after 1982. The economy of the xian will probably remain in the shadow of its more gifted neighbors, although in absolute terms the improvement will be substantial.

NOTES

1. The merger was dissolved in late 1981, and the two former xian of Gaoming and Heshan were reinstated. The effects of this reinstatement are not yet observable in the production patterns. See *Da Kung Bao*, February 14, 1982.

2. The Foshan District (Diqu), in which Gaohe is a xian, is one of the seven administrative divisions which together with Hainan form the province of Guangdong (Figure 2).

3. State purchase takes up only a portion of total production. Only figures of total fish production are available, however. See Figure 8.

4. Experimental stations have been set up in Gaohe to breed and to propagate species of livestock introduced from Europe through Hong Kong.

5. This directive is found in a document of the Chinese Communist Party (CCP). The contents of the document are discussed in two articles: *Beijing Review*, March 16, 1979, and *Beijing Review*, June 14, 1982. The title of the document is "Decision on Some Questions Concerning the Acceleration of Agricultural Development (Draft)," 1978. The document was adopted at the Third Plenary Session of the 11th Central Committee of the CCP in December 1978.

LITERATURE CITED

Beijing Review, 1979, (March 16), China to speed up agricultural development. pp. 8–9.

———, 1980, (February 4), On reforming the economic management system. pp. 16–21.

———, 1980, (November 10), Rural contract. pp. 5–6.

———, 1981, (January 19), Let some localities and peasants prosper first. pp. 19–22.

———, 1981, (March 16), System of responsibility in agricultural production. pp. 3–4.

———, 1982, (June 14), A program for current agricultural work. pp. 21–27.

Chan, Wahkong, 1977, *The central places of Kuang-tung Province.* University of Michigan unpublished Ph.D. thesis.

Chen, C.S., 1978, *Guangdong dizhi* (Geography of Guangdong). Hong Kong: Tienti Publishing House.

Da Gong Bao, 1982, (February 14), p. 3.

Hongqi (Red Flag), 1980, Nongye xiandaihua yu xiangcun zonghe fazhan (Agricultural modernization and integrated village development). No. 4, pp. 2–8.

———, 1981, Bishu shifen zhongshi liangshi wenti (We must consider thoroughly the grain problem). No. 5, pp. 24–26.

Hua, Guofeng, 1979, (July 18), Report on the work of the government. *Main Documents of the Second Session of the Fifth National People's Congress of the People's Republic of China.* Beijing: Foreign Language Press, pp. 5–100.

Liang, Ren-cai, 1956, *Guangdong jingji dili* (Economic geography of Guangdong). Beijing: Kexue Chubanshe.

Nanfang ribao (Southern Daily), 1981, (Sept. 14). Gaohe xian chuxian nongye shangwang xin zhumian (Agricultural production in Gaohe County shows recent improvement). p. 2.

_____ , 1981, (Oct. 2). Gaohe xian xiaping dukou zhian chingkuang haochuan (Domestic situation at Xiaping Ferry, Gaohe County is improving). p. 2.

Sun, Ching-chi, editor, 1959, *Huanan jingji dili* (Economic Geography of South China). Beijing: Kexue Chubanshe.

Xu, Jun-min, 1957, *Guangdong ziran dili tezheng* (Physical Geography of Guangdong). Guangzhou: Guangdong People's Press.

Xue, Muqiao, 1981, *China's Socialist Economy*. Beijing: Foreign Language Press.

Zhong, Ba Song and Wang, Guang Yao, 1958, Guanyu Zhujiang sanjiaozhou jige wenti (Some problems related to the Pearl River Delta). *Dili xue ziliao* (Memoirs of Geography), No. 3, pp. 11-22.

Zhong, Gongfu, 1980, Zhujiang sanjiaozhoude 'Sanji Yutang'—yige shuilu xianghu zuoyongde rengong shengtai xitong (Mulberry dyke fish pond on the Zhujiang delta—a complete artificial ecosystem of land-water interaction. *Acta Geographica Sinica (Dili xuebao)*, Vol. 35, No. 3, pp. 200-209.

Zhongguo Jiaotong Tuce (Atlas of Communications in China), 1979. Beijing: Ditu Chubanshe.

Urban Environmental Quality in China: A Luxury or a Necessity?

Sen-dou Chang

Deterioration of the quality of life in the urban environment is often attributed to a combination of factors: a rapid increase in population with a rise in per capita consumption of resources due to increased industrialization. In view of these factors, the People's Republic of China has been considered a country with few serious environmental problems. It reportedly has a relatively low percentage of urban population; a rigid policy of controlling rural–urban migration; and a practice of developing small-scale industries in rural, rather than urban, areas. There have been official declarations (voiced specifically at the International Environmental Conference in Stockholm in 1972) that few environmental problems exist under socialist leadership. Some specialists claim that China's socialist leadership may have provided a much needed alternative to developmental policies currently followed by many developing countries.

But such claims of success may not be justified. Since 1979 and with the start of the economic readjustment programs, China's news media as well as scholarly journals have revealed with astonishing openness and frankness a great deal of information concerning environmental problems in China. This paper, based upon current available information, is a brief survey of China's environmental problems in urban areas; the major causes of these problems; and their impact on China's modernization programs. An evaluation is also made of China's present policy for mitigating these problems.

82

AIR POLLUTION

Air quality in China's large cities ranks among the poorest in the world. Particulate levels have been measured to be approximately 10 times that of major urban areas of the United States. The emphasis on heavy industry as a priority in China's economic development program and the rapid development of chemical, metallurgical, petroleum, thermoelectric power, textile, printing and dyeing, and pulp and paper industries since 1949 have created a major pollution problem in China.

The total emission of particulate matter from both industrial plants and residential areas in China amounted to 14 million tons in 1980 as compared with 12 million t emitted in the United States in 1965, according to Wang (1981). The emission of sulfur dioxide totaled 15 million t in China in 1980 as compared with 26 million t emitted in the United States in 1965 (Wang, 1981). Fly ash and sulfur dioxide emitted in large quantities resulted mainly from the burning of coal, a primary residential cooking and heating fuel in Chinese cities.

This is especially so in the northern cities in the winter. In Beijing, for example, the amount of sulfur dioxide in the air in winter months is three times as high as in summer, whereas the amount of carbon monoxide is four times higher (Tai, 1980). High aggregates of sulfur dioxide and carbon monoxide in Beijing during the winter months are also attributed to a high incidence of temperature inversion; inversion occurs 85 percent of all days in winter as compared with 50 to 70 percent of the time in other seasons of the year (Tai, 1980). Beijing also recorded an increasing content of fly ash in the air. According to one estimate, the amount of fly ash in the urbanized area ranges from 25 tons per square kilometer per month in summer to 80 t/km^2/month in winter, averaging about 50 t/km^2/month for the year (Tai, 1980). A total of 390,000 t of particulates is contributed annually by coal burning for both industrial and residential uses. Coal burning is also responsible for issuing 260,000 t of sulfur dioxide annually in the city (Gao, 1980). The increasing content of fly ash in the air is the major cause of increasing frequency of both foggy days and smoggy days in the city.

During the period from 1971 to 1978, 150 more foggy days were observed than the period from 1961 to 1970 (Tai, 1980). The 1971–1978 period also witnessed 2,000 more smoggy days than the 1961–1970 period, a 50 percent increase (Tai, 1980). Coal burning in the city also produces an unknown amount of benzopyrene which is believed to be carcinogenic. The city's lung cancer death rate has increased about 30 percent during the 1974–1978 period (Tai, 1980).

Beijing is not the only major city in China with air pollution problems. Several other cities have the same or even worse problems, but they are seldom mentioned in Chinese news media or journals. The only data available concerning the extent of air pollution in major cities in China and the possible associated damages to human life and working days were compiled by the U.S. Environmental Protection Agency's delegation to China in October 1979, as shown in Table 1.

Evaluated with the maximum standards of 100 $\mu g/m^3$ for clean air set in California, three major cities in China—Shanghai, Wuhan, and Guangzhou—have surpassed the threshold by a great margin. The number of working days lost in the three cities appears to be proportionate to the total urban population in each city. Whereas the number of deaths cau' ad by suspended particles is a reflection of the nature of the particles, the amount of suspended particles ($\mu g/m^3$) is an indicator of the types of industries in different cities. Wuhan, a steel city in the middle of the Yangtze valley, has (ne highest death rate believed to be caused by suspended particles. Guangzhou, which is mainly a city of light industries, records the lowest death rate of the three cities.

Since 1978 China has extracted more than 600 million t of raw coal per year. Nearly one third of this output has been used as

TABLE 1

Content of Suspended Particles in Selected Chinese Cities, 1979

	Average suspended particles in 24 hours ($\mu g/m^3$)	Maximum content of suspended particles in 24 hours ($\mu g/m^3$)	General absenteeism of industrial workers per annum (1,000 days)	Number of deaths believed to be caused by air pollution per annum
Beijing	80	160	25,000	850
Shanghai	150	200	40,000	1,300
Wuhan	170	400	22,000	3,500
Guangzhou	190	190	20,000	700

Source: Qu, 1980.

household fuel, either as lump coal or coal-dust briquettes (Smil, 1980). Combustion of these raw fuels in small stoves is inefficient; only 10–18 percent of the chemical energy in coal is converted to useful thermal energy as opposed to 80–90 percent for large boilers used in the industrialized nations. The pollutants are released without much dispersion, very low above the ground, making for a most intractable air quality problem—especially in China's northern cities (Smil, 1980).

Industrial coal combustion is an equally serious contributor to China's air pollution. In Beijing, where more than 8 million t of coal are consumed annually, 72 percent of the fuel burned in industrial enterprises is wasted due to boiler inefficiencies. Low (30–40 percent) efficiencies are typical for most of the country (Smil, 1980). Consequently, in a single year only about 180 million t of the more than 600 million t of total coal output were converted to useful thermal energy (*Renmin ribao*, May 13, 1979, p. 3). It was estimated by some energy specialists in China that improving the combustion efficiency in China's numerous outdated thermal power plants and industrial boilers could reduce particulate and gaseous emissions by as much as 50 percent (*Renmin ribao*, May 13, 1979, p. 3). Obligatory installation of electrostatic precipitators would virtually eliminate gross black smoke still polluting the atmosphere in many Chinese cities. Pollution-control equipment in China is almost nonexistent, and the development of a pollution-control industry is just beginning. Chinese officials recently informed one Western businessman that among China's 400,000 enterprises only 200–300 electrostatic precipitators are in operation, and these are of uncertain efficiency (Weil, 1981). In the city of Nanjing, an industrial city of the lower Yangtze valley, only one quarter of the 724 furnaces and boilers are equipped with electrostatic precipitators. With recordings of carbon monoxide often reaching 1.5–2.1 $\mu g/m^3$ and particulates at 0.13–0.30 $\mu g/m^3$ Nanjing is one of the worst polluted cities in the nation (*Huanjing baohu*, 1981).

WATER RESOURCES

The rapid expansion of energy, metallurgical, and chemical industries, and the growth of cities have contributed to widespread water pollution in the densely populated areas of China. More than 90 percent of liquid municipal wastes and industrial wastes flow into various drainage systems without any kind of treatment. The

Huanghe drainage system in north China receives industrial and mining wastes totaling approximately 1 million t per day, whereas the Yangtze system carries 26 million t of industrial and urban wastes per day (*Huanjing baohu*, 1981). During winter months when the water level of the Yangtze is low, nearly one quarter of the river's total length below the steel city of Dukou in Sichuan Province is visibly polluted (*Huanjing baohu*, 1981). Pollution is evident in the different shades of color in the water. As a consequence of the pollution, the fish catch from the river has declined approximately 45 percent in the 16-year period from 1959 to 1975 (*Huanjing baohu*, 1981). For the nation as a whole the fish catch in fresh waters has shown astonishing decline from about 600,000 t annually in the 1950s to 400,000 t in the 1960s, and further to about 300,000 t in the 1970s.[1] Both industrial wastes and agricultural chemicals have contributed to such a sharp decline of freshwater fish catch in the past 30 years.

One of the important causes for widespread water pollution in China has been a lack of appropriate treatment of industrial wastes in both solid and liquid forms. It was estimated that the industrial sector releases more than 400 million t of solid wastes annually, and only a small fraction of this amount has been reused for production and construction purposes (Qu, 1980). In the past three decades, for example, there has been an accumulation of more than 1 billion t of tailings in the vicinities of coal mines throughout the country. These tailings occupy tens of thousands of hectares of productive land (Qu, 1980). Without appropriate storage or cover, harmful chemicals have been washed by rain and have drained into rivers and lakes or have seeped into the groundwaters. Ashes dumped into various drainage systems from thermoelectric power plants amount to 14 million t annually, a major cause of water pollution in the vicinity of large industrial cities (Qu, 1980).

For the nation as a whole, China is fairly well endowed with water resources. With a total surface runoff of 2,600 billion m^3 per year, China ranks third in available water resources among all nations in the world. In terms of per capita share, however, China's 2,700 m^3 fall far below the world average of 10,000 m^3 (Qu, 1980). With the seasonal concentration of rainfall in summer and the geographical concentration south of the Yangtze, more than 30 cities in China either completely or chiefly rely on groundwater for their water supply. As both industrialization and urbanization generate an increasing demand for water, especially in North China, excessive tapping of groundwater is a widespread phenomenon. For example, beneath the Beijing area is an aquifer of ancient fluvial fan origin.

Composed of sand and gravel and deposited by the Yungding River, this aquifer has the computed capability of storing and recharging 650 million t of water annually. In the past few years, however, 900 million t of water have been pumped each year from the Beijing area's aquifer for industrial and residential use. Excessive water withdrawal has resulted in groundwater subsidence at the rate of 1-1.5 m per year (*Renmin ribao*, November 11, 1979). In the early 1950s the groundwater level in the eastern suburb was only 1-3 m below the surface; now it is 20-30 m below (*Renmin ribao*, November 11, 1979). Likewise, the groundwater level in the western suburb has also lowered approximately 10 m. Because the groundwater level is low, stronger and more expensive equipment is needed, and there is a higher operational cost for water pumping. It has been estimated that the lower groundwater level and the hardening of the water quality have cost the state more than 200 million yuan annually (*Renmin ribao*, November 11, 1979).

Since the early 1950s Shanghai has experienced consistent ground subsidence. The first deep well to tap groundwater in Shanghai was dug in 1860, but it was not until 1921 that ground subsidence was first noticed. With the rapid industrial development in the First Five Year Plan (1952-1957), there was an increasing demand for groundwater. The flat plain upon which Shanghai developed was gradually transformed into a large saucer due to subsidence with the lowest point 2.37 m below the normal level (*Shanghai dili qianhua*, 1974, p. 78). As the general level of Shanghai is only 4 m above mean sea level, such a subsidence of both ground level and groundwater level easily induced seawater intrusion and tidal water pollution in Shanghai.

After several years of data gathering and map analysis, Shanghai's hydrologists have found that there is a definite correlation between the rate of ground subsidence and the rate of the lowering of groundwater levels. Simultaneous periodic injection of water into all deep wells in a concerted effort has been determined to be an efficient way to control ground subsidence. As both industrial and residential consumption of groundwater peaks in summer months, the injection of water to the ground must be done in winter months. The first large-scale water injection was carried out in the winter of 1966 and resulted in the elevation of the groundwater level by more than 10 m, as compared with 1965. This water injection was accompanied by a 6 mm rise in the ground level (*Shanghai dili qianhua*, 1974, p. 95). The injection of relatively cold water in winter months into a permeable stratum, 75-150 m below ground level, keeps the water temperature constantly at 19 °C. This water temperature is not only welcomed by users in the residential areas in the summer but is most beneficial to urban cotton textile industries in regulating workshop temperature and humidity (*Shanghai dili qianhua*, 1974, p. 90). At this time the subsidence of ground level in Shanghai is basically under control. What is not known, however, is whether a cost-benefit analysis was made of this interesting operation.

In addition to the gradual diminishing of groundwater resources, most large cities have also experienced increasing groundwater pollution. One scientist estimates that among the largest 44 cities in the nation, 41 have serious groundwater pollution problems of various degrees (*Huanjing baohu*, 1980a). The most common pollutants are phenol, arsenic, chlorides, mercury, cyanide, chromic acid, and nitrate, all from untreated industrial wastes (*Huanjing baohu*, 1980a). A widespread phenomenon in the urban areas of China is the increasing hardening of groundwater. In the Beijing area, for example, the hardness of the groundwater has been increasing at the rate of 0.5–1 degrees (expressed as 10 mg/per liter CaO) annually in recent years. Within an area of 200 km^2 the hard water measured has already surpassed 25 degrees, the recommended threshold for drinkable water set by the national standard (*Renmin ribao*, November 11, 1979).

LAND RESOURCES

Loss of productive farmland to the rapid space-demanding worldwide urbanization process has alarmed those who study food-famine processes. China, a nation with only 1.5 mu (about 0.1 ha) of cultivated land per capita, can little afford to lose productive cropland. In 1957 China's cultivated area was 1.677 billion mu, or 111.8 million ha, but in 1977 many Chinese sources list just 1.49 billion mu, or only 100 million ha. The data provided imply a loss of 180 million mu (12 million ha) or 12 percent of farmland in just over two decades, equivalent to the total amount of cultivated land of Sichuan, Guangdong, and Guangxi combined (*Renmin ribao*, April 29, 1980).

While some farmland has been lost to natural processes such as soil erosion and landslides, much of the land lost was a result of conversion to urban and industrial land use. Beijing in the early 1950s, for example, reported 9.11 million mu (607,340 ha) of cultivated area in the municipality. After 30 years of urban expansion, only 6.40 million mu (426,700 ha) still remained in 1980

(*Renmin ribao*, April 29, 1980). In three decades nearly thirty percent of Beijing's cultivated land has disappeared. According to records kept by the Beijing Municipal Statistics Office, national enterprise units and institutes of the central government have been responsible for 68 percent of the drafted land. Most often the land converted to urban use was productive vegetable-growing farmland owned by communes in the suburban counties of the municipality (*Renmin ribao*, April 29, 1980). There has been a shortage of vegetables in Beijing in recent years, and each year the shortage increases.

Emphasis has been placed upon providing living quarters for urban residents, and the process of converting agricultural land for housing construction has been accelerated. In Tianjin, for example, 1,400 mu of land (nearly 100 ha) were requisitioned in 1978 by the city for construction of residential units. Again in 1979, 14,000 mu of land (nearly 1,000 ha) belonging to 23 brigades were requisitioned, and the brigades were compensated with a fee of 16.81 million yuan (approximately $11 million) paid by the city authority. Consequently, six brigades had their organizational rights revoked on grounds of lack of arable land. More than 40,000 people engaged in food-producing agriculture activities were compelled to move and be assigned to nonagricultural jobs (*Renmin ribao*, November 28, 1980).

Loss of good agricultural land to urban construction is also a phenomenon around provincial towns and county seats. In the province of Jiangxi, for example, the total agricultural land has declined from more than 40 million mu (2.67 million ha) in the early 1950s to 38 million mu (2.54 million ha) in 1979 (*Quanming ribao*, June 9, 1979). In the same period, due to population increase, the per capita share of cultivated land in the province has declined from 2.7 mu (0.45 acre) to 1.2 mu (0.2 acre) (*Quanming ribao*, June 9, 1979). Most of the lost land is in the category of "high and stable yield land" which constitutes only one quarter of the total cultivated land in China.

There are at least two relevant factors that might explain why China has been losing good farmland so rapidly to urban construction. First, it has been due to either national policy or local practice that urban development in Chinese cities since 1949 has mainly occurred in the outer fringes of existing cities. The old city urban cores have not been systematically renewed or renovated for new urban land uses. Lack of multistory buildings in urban construction has also been a cause for conversion of more agricultural land. Second, the promotion of small local industries during the Cultural Revolution has greatly stimulated the growth of agricultural-related industries in almost every county. Without proper regional planning, many of these industries have been located in the outskirts of county towns, often on prime agricultural land of the county. Uncontrolled construction of collective enterprises and rural housing in the communes or brigades in recent years has also been a cause for shrinkage of good farmland. The decentralization of land-use policy decision-making down to the lowest rural level in recent years may not be conducive to alleviating this perilous problem in China.

WASTE DISPOSAL

With an extremely high man–land ratio and with a disparity between population and resource endowment, the Chinese have been known traditionally for their thrifty and ingenious ways of recycling resources. In the past three decades, however, the rapid pace of industrialization and urbanization has created a series of environmental problems far beyond the controlling capacity of traditional ways of resource recycling in an agrarian economy. One of the most serious environmental problems facing China today is the country's limited capability to handle the enormous amount of industrial wastes in large cities, the main cause of environmental deterioration throughout China. Most of these wastes are left on the open grounds near the industrial or mining sites, often occupying thousands of hectares of productive land and causing much water contamination in the vicinity. While some cities have processed these wastes for use in road construction or in cement manufacturing, the great bulk of these wastes remains untreated and will be a pollution threat to soils and waters for years to come.

The liquid wastes released by industrial units in various cities are a more perilous problem than solid wastes. In the municipality of Beijing, for example, about 1.35 billion t of water are consumed by industries annually (Gao, 1980). Of this amount only thirty percent is reused by industries, and a smaller amount is treated for agricultural or residential use (Gao, 1980). There are nearly 2 million t of waste water dumped daily into the limited drainage system in the area. This contaminates the rivers in the suburbs so badly that neither fish nor shrimp have been caught recently in the counties immediately surrounding the city. It was estimated that the damages in agriculture caused by polluted waters in the vicinity of Beijing amount to 4 million yuan annually (Gao, 1980).

Shanghai, the city with a concentration of more industrial

enterprises than any other Chinese city, faces a proportionate problem in water pollution due to industrial wastes. The city discharges a total of 6.2 million t of waste water daily, including 5 million t of industrial wastes and 1.2 million t of residential wastes (Xu, 1980). Of this amount, more than 4 million t are directly discharged into the Huangpu River without any treatment. The daily discharge of the Huangpu is 12 million t of water during the dry season (Xu, 1980). Thus, as much as one third of the total daily flow of the Huangpu in winter months is contributed by industrial wastes alone. Impact of the contaminated river water is not confined to Shanghai Municipality. The contaminated water drains into the estuary of the Yangtze and, through daily rising tides, reaches as far as Zhenjiang and Yangzhou more than 250 km upstream (Xu, 1980). It was estimated that a little more than 200,000 t of waste water in Shanghai is treated daily either by municipal water treatment plants or by facilities set up by individual industrial units (*Renmin ribao*, November 14, 1979). In addition to 4 million t of waste water discharging to the Huangpu, contaminated water is also discharged either to the Yangtze or to the East China Sea directly through two water pipes extended from the western and southern districts of the city (*Renmin ribao*, November 14, 1979).

In China water-treatment facilities use mainly mechanical separation, flotation, sedimentation, and biological treatment. More sophisticated processes such as ion exchange and reverse osmosis as practiced in industrialized countries are rare in China, though either one of these processes is a component of some imported plants. Chinese researchers are trying to save money by developing indigenous low-cost technologies. For example, a petrochemical plant has initiated a pilot project that uses local algae grown in lakes to remove petrochemical waste from refinery effluents. It is also reported that ducks were used in an attempt to purify wastewater discharge by petrochemical plants in Beijing and Shanghai. It is not known, however, how effective these two attempts are in improving water quality.

In terms of the control of waste disposal through smoke or exhaust stacks, China's air pollution control technology is based primarily on that used in the Soviet Union in the 1950s, and the control of particulates appears to be taking precedence over other emissions, including sulfur dioxide. Electrostatic precipitators and wet scrubbers are manufactured only in small quantities, often on a makeshift basis by plants that use them. Efficiencies as low as 70 percent were reported in some cases (Weil, 1981).

NOISE POLLUTION

Of all the environmental problems in Chinese cities, noise pollution is probably the most readily noticed by foreign visitors. With the increasing number of motor vehicles in the streets combined with construction projects in both industrial districts and residential areas, noise pollution is rapidly becoming the most annoying urban problem in China. Experimental monitoring of noise levels started as early as 1973 in the city of Beijing (Cheng, 1980). A few years later between 1975 and 1977 another seven cities initiated city-wide noise level monitoring (Cheng, 1980). Table 2 shows a comparison of the level of noise pollution (L_{NP}) and traffic noise index (TNI) between selected Chinese cities and cities in Western countries.[2] As noise pollution in urban areas is largely contributed by moving vehicles on the street, it is rather surprising to find such a high level of noise pollution in China. China has relatively fewer vehicles, proportional to the urban population, on the streets than most countries at a comparable level of economic development. The city of Beijing has only about 140,000 vehicles, for example, but the noise level in the city is generally 9 db higher than that of Tokyo, a city possessing more than 2 million vehicles (Yu et al., 1980). The following factors seem to have contributed jointly to the higher level of noise pollution in Chinese cities.

TABLE 2

TL_{NP} and TNI of Selected Cities

(Unit: db)

City	L_{NP}	TNI	City	L_{NP}	TNI
Guangzhou	95	108	Hong Kong	80	87
Hangzhou	111	143	London	74	68
Chongqing	106	132	Madrid	89	89
Wuhan	109	136	Medford, Mass.	69	69
Nanjing	105	127	New York	88	96
Harbin	95	137	Rome	90	88

Source: Ko, 1978.

Excessive Use of Horns by Drivers of Vehicles

This is a common phenomenon in many Asian countries, and China is no exception. A survey conducted at Xidan Road junction, a busy traffic area in Beijing, reveals that a frequency of horn-blowing of up to 16 times a minute has been recorded (Zhang, 1981). Both the need to manipulate through roads crowded with large numbers of pedestrians during the day and the fact that the horns rather than headlights are used in the evening have contributed to a high frequency of horn-blowing in Chinese cities. It has been noted in Beijing that a driver blowing his vehicle's horn at the normal moving speed on a busy street would raise the noise level from the background noise by 7 db (Ma, 1981).

Poor Maintenance and Old Age of Vehicles

Age and poor maintenance are especially a problem with municipal buses in most Chinese cities and with old-style tramcars moving on rails in large cities in the northeast. A shortage of trained mechanics, inadequacy of equipment in repair shops, and the laxity of regulations on inspections of vehicles have contributed to the poor maintenance of moving vehicles in China.

Many Small Tractors Hauling Farm Products

A large number of small hand tractors hauling both passengers and agricultural products from rural areas is a common scene in Chinese cities, especially a few hours after midnight when suburban communes and brigades haul agricultural products to urban markets. This phenomenon is a prime contributing factor to noise pollution and is responsible for high levels of noise pollution in Chinese cities throughout the entire 24 hours of a day. Constant high levels of noise pollution during both day and night are characteristic of Chinese cities—more so than most cities in any nation of the world.

ENVIRONMENTAL POLICIES IN CHINA

In spite of the denial of environmental problems in China at the First International Conference on Human Environment held in Stockholm in 1972, China's first air and water standards were promulgated in 1963. They were copied almost verbatim from the Soviet Union (Weil, 1981). Compared to environmental standards in the Western countries, Chinese standards are significantly lax. Although the country's first antipollution administrative organ, the Environmental Protection Office, was formed in 1973 under direct state council jurisdiction, its standards are seldom seriously enforced.

The first sign that the Environmental Protection Office might be given some real power came in 1979 with the "trial" implementation of the first national law on environmental protection. This law, covering land use and plant and animal protection, as well as industrial pollution, was more a sweeping statement of principle than a concrete program. It did stipulate that factories must meet emission standards; that the state has the right to levy fines against, force the relocation of, or even close offending plants; and finally, that Environmental Protection Offices be established at local levels (Jin, 1980). However, no guidelines for its enforcement were provided, nor was it indicated how environmental standards would be interpreted.

National standards in China are now being jointly formulated by the Environmental Protection Office, the Health Ministry, and Industrial Ministries. In the meantime, provincial and municipal level units have been encouraged to devise more specific regulations to meet the local needs. Many have already done so. The following measures appear to be the current policy in alleviating pollution problems in China and in implementing environmental regulations in most cities.

Plant Closing or Relocation

Due to the virtual absence of urban planning in China, many polluting factories are situated in the middle of cities and residential neighborhoods. In recent years there has been growing pressure to relocate them in satellite towns of large municipalities, to force them to close, or to persuade them to switch to nonpolluting product lines. According to one report, 167 plants nationwide have been threatened with shutdown if pollution is not alleviated (Weil, 1981). An important target of these efforts is the world-renowned

94

tourist city of Guilin, which was unwisely developed into an industrial city. Twelve plants, including metallurgical works, were closed, and 17 are scheduled to be moved (Weil, 1981).

Concerns have also been expressed regarding the serious deterioration of the environmental quality of the capital city of Beijing, a cultural center of China which has been transformed unwisely into one of the most significant heavy industrial cities of North China in the past three decades. In a "four-point" circular published in April 1980 the Central Committee called for a halt to the rapid industrialization of the capital area and for its restoration as a political and cultural center. By August 1980, 5 factories had moved out of town, 40 had merged with others in the outskirts, and 43 had switched to nonpolluting product lines (Weil, 1981). An equivalent number of plants reportedly were contemplating similar steps. Dramatic evidence of the government's determination was its November 1980 decision to cancel construction of the Dongfang Chemical Works in Beijing's eastern suburbs, despite the fact that construction had begun and contracts for equipment had been signed with Japanese firms (Weil, 1980). The danger posed to the area's groundwater, the primary source for 2 million Beijing residents, was apparently a main factor in the cancellation.

Fines

The imposition of fines on the polluting units is based on the theory that polluting the environment is a social cost, and that society should be compensated by the polluting units. Since the new regulations went into effect, according to the Environmental Protection Office, more than 1,500 factories have been assessed fines by various administrative bodies (Weil, 1981). The largest known fine, the equivalent to $1.3 million, was collected by the Hubei provincial government from a large copper complex near Daye (Weil, 1981). Suzhou, a city in Jiangsu Province, has been the vanguard in setting up standards and procedures for fine imposition. A basic formula for fine assessment used in Suzhou is: the amount of the fine = the volume of wastes (in tons or in cubic meters) × the amount of pollutants exceeding the national standards (in percentage) × the standard fee for each unit of waste which exceeds the national standard (*Huanjing baohu*, 1980b). In Suzhou the standard fee for each ton of polluted water containing excessive mercury, cyanide, lead, phenol, arsenic, or organic phosphate is 0.20 yuan; for that discharged by a paper mill—0.50 yuan; for each ton of coal burned and releasing black smoke—5 yuan; and for that of oil—10 yuan (*Huanjing baohu*, 1980b). With the imposition of the responsibility system on every plant for industrial production in recent years, such an assessment seems to be working effectively, as the accumulation of large fines for a particular industrial unit diminishes the amount of the year-end bonus each worker shares. Thus, it is basically a material incentive policy imposed on the rank and file of an enterprise for a more efficient industrial management in a socialist political system.

Antipollution Equipment in New Plants

A November 1980 circular issued by the Environmental Protection Office and the State Planning, Economic, and Capital Construction Commissions mandates that funds for environmental protection equipment be listed as a line item in estimated, budgeted, and final accounts for all projects under the state plan. Also, it requires that the state organs inspecting completed projects not allow them to go into production without effective pollution-control equipment (Weil, 1981).

Another result of legislation was the 1979 formation of the "General Machinery Technical Corporation" under the First Ministry of Machine Building. This corporation reportedly is led by competent and informed engineers who hope to win orders from Chinese enterprises to build air and water treatment equipment. This corporation can be said to represent the beginning of an antipollution industry in China. In the meantime, all imported foreign plants are required to have, as part of the purchasing contract, modern antipollution equipment which Chinese technology at the present level may not be able to produce (Weil, 1981).

Monitoring Systems and Treatment Projects

Preparations are underway to build a national environmental monitoring system which will eventually include 290 monitoring stations throughout China (Guo, 1981). So far, a total of 172 monitoring stations have been built along the Yangtze and its tributaries (Guo, 1981). In addition, 16 monitoring stations and 145 monitoring points have been set up along the coast (Guo, 1981). A number of stations have been established along the Huanghe and the Huaihe. It appears that water quality analysis is the prior task of the monitoring stations in operation.

96

An increasing number of water treatment projects are under construction, although their size and capability are difficult to assess. In 1979 the province of Hunan, for example, embarked on a program to build 335 water treatment projects in factories and cities along the Xiang River. Reportedly the Hunan project will reduce the amount of untreated water by more than 100 million m^3. In addition, a number of cities, including Beijing, Shanghai, and Xi'an, are either planning or constructing municipal secondary water treatment facilities (Weil, 1981).

International Exchanges

In the past few years China has initiated contacts with academics, firms, and government agencies of a few selected countries to become more familiar with approaches to pollution control. The U.S. Environmental Protection Agency has signed a protocol with the Environmental Protection Office calling for cooperation in environmental health research, pollution control, and research into environmental processes and effects, and the U.S. EPA is negotiating cooperation in environmental impact assessment studies. A tentative agreement has been reached to carry out joint studies of the epidemiological effects of residential coal burning in Yunnan Province, and organic contamination of drinking water in Shanghai (Weil, 1981). Joint studies on the flow of pollutants from one place to another are also under discussion. By an agreement with the United Nations Environment Program (UNEP) and the World Health Organization (WHO) in 1981, the Wuhan section of the Yangtze, the Jinan section of the Huanghe, and the Gaoyao section of the Zhujiang as well as Taihu Lake, have been put under the world water quality monitoring system of these two world organizations (Guo, 1981).

In October 1980 a delegation from the East-West Center's Environmental and Policy Institute in Honolulu visited China for two weeks at the invitation of China's Environmental Protection Office and conducted a workshop in Beijing with top Chinese environmental scientists. The environmental group from the East-West Center will render aid to Chinese scientists in an attempt to gain new concepts, new analytical approaches, and new types of professionals to deal with environmental aspects of China's modernization programs (*Intrachange*, 1980). Annual workshops will be conducted in Beijing and in Honolulu in the next few years.

CONCLUSIONS AND PROSPECTS

The environmental quality of urban areas in a developing country is closely associated with the priorities set in the economic development programs, the management skills of large enterprises, the sophistication of science and technology, and most important of all, the general awareness of the populace of an ecologically concerned value system. Recent accelerated environmental deterioration within Chinese cities is a reflection of the inefficiency in utilization of China's major energy resource, coal; the inadequacy of sewage systems in urban areas; the low level of recycling and treatment of industrial waters; the employment of obsolete equipment in industrial production and in transportation; and the failure to set up pollution control measures during more than three decades of rapid industrialization in both urban and rural areas.

Since the economic readjustment programs initiated in 1979, the Chinese leadership has come a long way in changing its attitude toward development policy; in setting up institutions; and in formulating legal procedures to mitigate environmental problems throughout the country. However, causes of environmental deterioration in urban areas of China, as mentioned above, will not disappear overnight. Moreover, with so many priorities in the modernization programs, it is unlikely within the foreseeable future that China will allocate, like many developed countries, more than 1 percent of her gross national product to curb environmental pollution. The current environmental policy in China seems to be a correction of past mistakes in industrial location and in unplanned land uses as well as an emphasis on self-reliance on the part of large enterprises in solving pollution problems. City planning, expansion of green areas, and urban renewal schemes are also considered as an essential part of environmental improvement programs in many cities (Chen, 1980). With limited resources available for environmental control in such a vast nation, national decision-makers are setting top environmental protection priorities in a few large cities, such as Beijing and Tianjin, and a few scenic cities frequented by foreign tourists, such as Hangzhou, Suzhou, and Guilin. Strides already have been made toward the improvement of air and water qualities in Beijing and Guilin.

But for most cities in China environmental quality likely will deteriorate in the near future before getting better in a longer perspective. Like many other developing countries in Asia striving for industrialization and for material improvement, a clean and quiet urban environment may still be considered a "luxury" in measuring the quality of Chinese life.

NOTES

1. The share of freshwater fish in Chinese fisheries has fallen from 40 percent in 1959 to 23 percent in 1978. See *Renmin ribao*, April 5, 1979, p. 2 and May 18, 1981, p. 2. See also *Huanjing baohu*, 1980c, No. 3, p. 6.

2. The value of TNI is derived from the equation $TNI = L_{90} + 4d - 30$ db, where L_{90} denotes the minimum noise level recorded more than 90 percent of the time; L_{10} denotes the minimum noise level recorded 10 percent of the time; and $d = L_{10} - L_{90}$. L_{NP} is derived from the equation $L_{NP} = L_{50} + d + d_{60}^{2}$ db. See Ko, 1978.

LITERATURE CITED

Chen, Chuankong, 1980, Chengshi guahua yu huanjing baohu (Urban planning and environment protection). In *Huanjing kexue yanjiu yu jinzhan* (Research and Progress of Environmental Science). Beijing: Kexue Chubanshe, pp. 346-355.

Cheng, Mingkun, 1980, Woguo chengshi jaosheng xianzhuang ji kongzhi jianyi (Urban noise in our country and suggestions for controlling it). In *Huanjing kexue yanjiu yu jinzhan* (Research and Progress of Environmental Science). Beijing: Kexue Chubanshe, pp. 228-242.

Gao, Yusheng, 1980, Chengshi huanjing baohu de guihua yu shisi (Planning and practice of urban environmental protection). *Huanjing baohu* (Environmental Protection). No. 4, pp. 3-7.

Guo, Huanxuan, 1981, Environmental protection in China. *Beijing Review*, (June 29), Vol. 24, No. 26, pp. 12-15.

Huanjing baohu, 1980a, Woguo chengshi gongshui zhong de huanjing dizhi wenti (Problems concerning environmental geology in supplying waters to our cities). *Huanjing baohu*, No. 1, pp. 4-5, 35.

_____ , 1980b, Paiwu shefei shi huanjing guanli de yixiang zhongyao choushi (Collecting fees for waste discharges is an important measure in environmental management). *Huanjing baohu*, No. 2, pp. 8-10.

_____ , 1980c, No. 3, p. 6.

_____ , 1981, Baohu dajiang dahe yanan de shuicheng (Protection of riverine cities along the Changjiang and the Huanghe). *Huanjing baohu*, No. 1, pp. 14-16.

Intrachange (News for the East-West Center Community), 1980, (November 7), Vol. 1, No. 20, p. 1.

Jin, Ruilin, 1980, Woguo huanjing baohufa de jiben yuanzhe he shisi zhong de jige wenti (Basic principles and some implementation problems of our environmental protection laws). *Huanjing baohu*, No. 1, pp. 6-9.

Ko, N.W.M., 1978, Traffic noise in a high rise city. *Applied Acoustics*, Vol. 11, pp. 225-239.

Ma, Dayou, 1981, Zaosheng huanjing. *Huanjing baohu*, No. 1, pp. 4-7.

Qu, Geping, 1980, Gongye shengchan yu huanjing baohu (Industrial production and environmental protection). *Huanjing baohu* (Environmental Protection), No. 2, pp. 3-6.

Quanming ribao (Quanming Daily), 1979, (June 9), p. 4.

Renmin ribao (People's Daily), 1979, (April 5), p. 2.

_____ , 1979, (May 13), p. 3.

_____ , 1979, (November 11), p. 2.

_____ , 1979, (November 14), p. 2.

_____ , 1980, (April 29), p. 5.

_____ , 1980, (November 28), p. 2.

_____ , 1981, (May 18), p. 2.

Shanghai dili qianhua (Geographical Survey of Shanghai), 1974. Shanghai: Renmin Chubanshe.

Smil, Vaclav, 1980, Environmental degradation in China. *Asian Survey*, Vol. 20, No. 8, pp. 777-778.

Tai, Qisheng, 1980, Beijing daqi wulan de tedian ji gaishan jianyi (The characteristics of air pollution in Beijing and corrective measures). *Huanjing baohu*, No. 6, pp. 5-ò.

Wang, Huabin, 1981, Zhanwang bashiniandai woguo chenxiang jiangzhu de fazhen (Prospects of urban and rural construction for our country in the 1980s). *Jianzhu xuebao* (Architectural Journal), No. 1, pp. 15-23.

Weil, Martin, 1981, Cleaning up China's environment. *China Business Review*, Vol. 8, No. 1, pp. 50-54.

Xu, Dixin, 1980, Shixian sihua yu shengtai jingji xue (Four modernizations and ecological economies). *Jingji yanjiu* (Economic Research), November, pp. 14-18.

Yu, Guangyuan et al., 1980, *Lun Huanjing Guanli* (Essays on Environmental Management). Taiyuan: Shanxi Renmin Chubanshe, p. 21.

Zhang, Changling, 1981, Beijing shi qiche laba shenxue biaozhun di tantao (On the level of noise contributed by the automobile horns in the city of Beijing). *Huanjing baohu*, No. 2, pp. 29-31.

Water Resources Development and Its Environmental Impact in Beijing[1]

Laurence J.C. Ma
Liu Changming

The demand for water in the city of Beijing (Peking), China's capital and second largest metropolis, sharply increased in the last three decades as a result of rapid population growth and urban economic development. From 1949 to 1978 the supply of water in urban Beijing increased by 45 times, but the increase does not meet the city's current demand for water. The problem of water supply was particularly acute in the summers of 1981–82 as north China experienced a severe drought, which dried up all medium sized and small reservoirs and forced the large-scale Miyun Reservoir to stop water delivery completely (*Beijing ribao*, August 29, 1981, p. 1). Relative to the conditions of water supply in the city 30 years ago, Beijing today faces a more acute problem of water shortage.

Despite serious efforts by the Chinese government to contain the growth of Beijing, the city's population in mid-1980 reached 8.8 million (5.04 million in urban population and 3.76 million in rural population) (*Beijing ribao*, October 17, 1980, p. 1). The lack of effective long-range planning for the city's growth resulted in a variety of problems in the last three decades. The problems include

102

severe housing shortage, congestion, deteriorating environmental quality, and inadequate urban services and facilities (Ma, 1979). Such a criticism should not be construed as evidence that the city has not made progress in urban development. Indeed, many industrial and housing projects have drastically changed the city's landscape and brought a higher standard of living to a large number of people (Ma, 1981). Yet serious problems remain.

This paper examines the development of Beijing's water resources and the resultant environmental problems. The nation's policy of industrial development, which has fundamentally changed the morphology as well as the economic structure of China's large and medium-sized cities, will also be analyzed as the policy applies to Beijing and the use of the city's water resources.

PHYSICAL BASE

Climatologically, Greater Beijing is a water-deficient region. The area receives only a modest amount of precipitation, averaging 626 mm per year, more than 85 percent of which is concentrated in July, August, and September. The average annual potential evapotranspiration in the area is approximately 900 mm. So, the annual deficit is about 300 mm. December and January are the driest months, and precipitation in the spring accounts for only 10 percent of the annual total. Annual total precipitation varies greatly. The difference between the wet and dry years can be as great as six times. In most years the farmland suffers from drought in the spring and is waterlogged in the fall.

Greater Beijing is located between 114°41'E–116°30'E and 39°25'N–40°25'N, in a total area of 16,800 km^2, 61 percent of which is hilly. There are 6.4 million mu (426,700 hectares) of agricultural land, 80 percent of which is irrigated (Investigation Group, 1981, p. 25). The city is situated at the northern apex of the North China Plain, surrounded in the north by the Jundu Shan (part of the Yan Shan) and in the west by the Xi Shan (part of the Taihang Shan). The topography of Greater Beijing drops gently from the northwest to the southeast. There are more than 40 rivers and streams in Greater Beijing, the larger ones being the Yongdinghe, Chaobaihe, and the Grand Canal (Figure 1). But the rivers are inadequate for providing the city's water supply. Beijing must rely on groundwater as a source for its water supply.

The Yongdinghe is the largest river in the city region, although

Figure 1

the area drained by the river in Beijing forms only a small part of the river's total drainage area. Much of the drainage area lies outside of the city boundary. Above the Guanting Reservoir, the river has a drainage area of 43,400 km^2 that contributes water to the reservoir; below the reservoir the river drains only 1,600 km^2 in the city region.

The other major rivers of Beijing are the Chaobaihe and the Wenyuhe, which is linked to the northern Grand Canal. The Chaobaihe originates in the hilly areas of northern Hebei Province and flows to the southeast through Greater Tianjin. Its total drainage area is 19,560 km^2. The Wenyuhe flows through the level part of the city region and links with the northern Grand Canal.

Most of the surface streams of Beijing are small, and they

originate in hilly regions in the city's northwest. In terms of volume, the Yongdinghe and the Chaobaihe are the most important sources of surface water that could be used by Beijing. The Yongdinghe provides water to the Guanting Reservoir, where the average annual storage capacity is 700 million m^3. The Chaobaihe supplies water to the Miyun Reservoir, where the average annual storage capacity is 1.7 billion m^3. The water of the Miyun Reservoir, however, is shared by the cities of Beijing and Tianjin and by Hebei Province. Beijing is allotted less than 700 million m^3 of water per year, or about 15 percent of the water actually used.

The streams of the region are characterized by relatively small volumes of water with great seasonal variability. The river beds may be dry for long periods of time during the dry season. Such an uneven pattern of river runoff results from rainfall distribution and creates problems in water supply for Beijing's industrial, agricultural, and domestic uses.

The level parts of Beijing were formed by the alluvial and diluvial deposits of such rivers as the Yongdinghe and the Chaobaihe. The loose but thick Quaternary sedimentary deposits not only have a strong capacity to be infiltrated, they are also good aquifers containing much groundwater.

Precipitation and the infiltration by surface water in the hilly regions of Beijing are the major sources of water for groundwater recharge in the lowland areas of the city. According to studies conducted by Beijing's hydrologists, these two sources provide 83 percent of the potential yield of water contained in the shallow aquifers of the lowland. The remaining 17 percent is supplied by the underground horizontal flows from the hilly regions to the lowland (Liu and Xie, 1981).

Precipitation and surface water infiltration provide Beijing with approximately 2.5 billion m^3 of water, the equivalent of 382 mm in terms of depth. This amount is approximately 61 percent of the city's natural precipitation. Many major cities of the world are located near large rivers for better water supply and transportation, but Beijing has no major rivers nearby, and it has always relied on groundwater for water supply. Groundwater resources must be taken into consideration in any study of Beijing's growth. Since 1949, 84 reservoirs, including the Miyun and the Guanting Reservoirs, have been built in Beijing, and they have greatly helped regulate the city's water supply. These reservoirs, however, have not been as important as the groundwater in terms of the volume of water available and the reliability of supply. The Miyun and the Guanting Reservoirs yearly provide the city with about 1 billion m^3 of water, which is used mainly by suburban industries and agriculture.

WATER QUANTITY AND CONSUMPTION

Various government agencies in Beijing have attempted to estimate the total amount of water, both surface and groundwater, that may be available to the city. The estimates vary only slightly, and most agencies estimate that in an average year the total is approximately 4.5 billion m^3: 2 billion m^3 from surface sources and 2.5 billion m^3 from groundwater. In dry years, however, the total amount of water available may not be much more than 3.5 billion m^3.

The amount of water available is insufficient to meet the city's needs. In 1978, for example, a total of 4.67 billion m^3 of water were used in Greater Beijing; the bulk was used by agriculture in the city's nine rural counties (Figure 2). Agricultural water use has contributed significantly to the city's food supply by increasing the per unit productivity of the land. In the three decades from 1949 to 1979, the total acreage of the city's farmland devoted to grain production decreased by 1.65 million mu (110,000 hectares) because of urban and industrial development, but the per mu yield increased from 63 kg to 348.5 kg. The total grain production of the city in 1979 reached 17.28 million kg, which was 4.5 times higher than the total in 1949 (Investigation Group, 1981, p. 25). Of the 3 billion m^3 of water used for irrigation in 1978, 1.3 billion m^3 were surface water (largely from the Miyun and Guanting Reservoirs), and 1.7 billion m^3 were groundwater. However, more water is needed for irrigation to increase the productivity of more than a million mu (66,700 hectares) of land that has been used mainly for dry farming (Liu and Xie, 1981, p. 10).

Industrial water use has created more serious problems than other types of water use. As Figure 3 shows, the amount of water supplied by the water works of the city proper to support industrial development in the last three decades has risen sharply. In addition to the water supplied by the water works, many industries have their own wells which provide the bulk of the water used by industries. Eighty-one percent of the water consumed in the built-up area of the city is for industrial use. As the groundwater of the city and its suburbs is tapped beyond the capacity of natural replenishment, the levels of groundwater drop every year. In vast areas near the city proper, the groundwater tables are now more than 4 m lower than the original levels, the lowest being 20 m below the normal level (*Renmin ribao*, February 9, 1981, p. 2). Deep cones of depression are commonly found in areas where the groundwater has been tapped too heavily.

In the southeastern suburb of Beijing, where more than 300

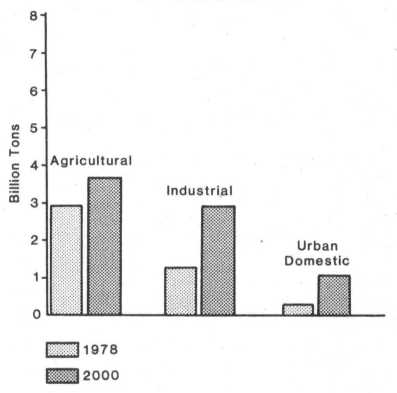

Figure 2

industries concentrate, the water table is dropping at the alarming rate of 1 m per year (Liu and Xie, 1981, p. 10). In an industrial zone in the eastern suburb, there are an average of 23 wells per km^2, or twice as many as is normally the case. Here a large cone of depression several hundred square kilometers in size formed, and land subsidence occurred (Zhu, 1980, p. 6). The effects and ramifications of the subsidence, however, have not been studied.

One problem of excessive tapping of the groundwater has been the increase of the water's hardness and mineral content. For example, the water of many wells in Beijing in the 1950s had a hardness of 10 degrees, but by the 1970s it increased to 20–30 degrees. The number of wells in which the water is unfit for drinking due to excessive hardness is increasing each year (Brigade of Hydrogeology, 1980, p. 38).

Domestic water consumption in urban Beijing rises steadily as the population of the city increases. Shortly after the 1949 revolution Beijing had a population of 2.03 million, with 1.65 million living in the urban districts (*Beijing Review*, 1980, p. 14). At present there are more than 5 million residents in urban Beijing. The average per capita consumption of water in urban Beijing is 145 l per day, but in high-quality apartment buildings the figure is between 300 and 450. In tourist hotels, such as the Beijing Hotel, the per capita consumption is as high as 2,000 l per day (Liu and Xie, 1981, pp. 10–11).

As the city's population continues to grow, as more new housing is built each year in the city (Ma, 1981, pp. 231–233), and as more and better tourist hotels with Western facilities are completed, the domestic demand for water in urban Beijing is bound to exceed the present level of consumption of 190 million m^3 per year (Figure 3). It has been estimated that Beijing will need 1 billion m^3 of water for domestic use by the year 2000. As the natural precipitation is already inadequate, and both the quantity and quality of the groundwater are declining, the prospect for the city to have a stable, sustained, and adequate water supply for domestic and industrial uses looks bleak. Unless remedial measures are taken immediately and implemented on a sustained basis, sooner or later the city will run out of water.

INDUSTRIAL DEVELOPMENT AND WATER POLLUTION

Urban Beijing has serious problems of water pollution as a consequence of the overdevelopment of heavy industry and the lack of effective actions on environmental protection. From 1949 to the end of 1978 the total investment for industrial development in Beijing amounted to 11.2 billion *yuan* (about $7 billion in 1981), of which 87.9 percent went to heavy industries. In terms of the value of industrial output, heavy industry in 1979 contributed 63.7 percent of the total value of 21 billion *yuan* ($13 billion), while light industry accounted for 36.3 percent (*Renmin ribao*, June 10, 1980, p. 2). Such high proportions in favor of heavy industry in Beijing exceed those of Shanghai, China's largest industrial city, and are

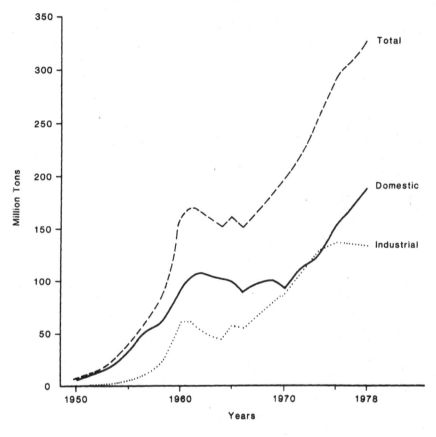

Figure 3

second only to those of Shenyang, the nation's leading iron and steel center (*Renmin ribao*, August 12, 1980, p. 2).

Beijing has about 3,700 factories of different sizes which employ a total of 1.4 million people. Approximately 28 percent of the city's urban population is employed by industries. Among the leading heavy industries are iron and steel industries and chemical engineering. There are more than 240 chemical industrial production units which employ 21 percent of the city's industrial labor force, occupy 22 percent of the city's industrial land, and produce 22 percent of the city's industrial value (*Renmin ribao*, September 1, 1980, p. 3). Most of the major industries are concentrated in either the city proper or its fringes. The city and its immediate hinterland, however, are not well endowed with natural resources. In addition to the shortage of water, raw materials such as coal, iron ore, and crude petroleum must be received from other places. Since Beijing is neither a riverine city nor a sea port, raw materials must be received by rail. Thus, not all of the necessary and sufficient conditions for the city to become a heavy industrial center are present. Even without industrial stimulus, Beijing will continue to grow as a political, cultural, and educational center.

The overdevelopment of heavy industry in Beijing has been caused by decisions made at the highest levels of economic planning, and such decisions have affected all large and medium-sized cities in China. Perhaps the most important policy that had the greatest impact on the urban landscape of China in the last three decades was "to transform consumer-cities into producer-cities," an ideologically attractive doctrine, which was proclaimed in early 1949 (*Renmin ribao*, March 17, 1949, p. 1) and which remained influential until 1980. The meaning of "consumer-cities (*xiaofei chengshi*)" has never been clearly defined, but "producer-cities (*shengchan chengshi*)" have during the years been used to represent cities with industries, especially heavy industries.

The emphasis on the development of heavy industry had its origin in the First Five-Year Plan (1953–57), which was formulated on the Soviet model of economic growth based on heavy industry. Except for the period of the Cultural Revolution (1966–69), heavy industry until 1980 was given top priority by China's planners. It was argued that only heavy industry could provide the equipment and technology needed by the other sectors of the economy and that it should be the core of China's program of economic development (Feng, Wan, and Zhang, 1980, p. 67).

Rapid industrial growth began in Beijing shortly after 1949 as the city attempted to become a "producer-city." During the Great Leap Forward (1958–60), the goal of the city was to be transformed into a "modern, socialist industrial base" in five years (Sha, 1980, p. 6). In 1977 planning policies called for the development of Beijing into an industrial center based on iron and steel, petrochemicals, electronics, and mechanical instruments (*Renmin ribao*, September 12, 1980, p. 5). The wisdom of such an emphasis on heavy industry was never questioned until 1980 when China began a serious effort to reassess the future directions of the nation's economic structure.

The priority placed on industrial growth in all Chinese cities carried the connotation that only industrial development could symbolize socialist economic growth. The construction of more and bigger factories and the achievement of higher production goals by

110

the industries became the only major concerns of the national as well as the local urban planners. The desires to establish more industries and to make large and medium-sized cities "producer-cities" were so strong that a large number of industrial projects were constructed without first giving careful consideration to the requirements for energy, transportation, resources (including water), and to the potential environmental impact. In many cases factories were built in the cities by ministries of industries of the State Council against the wishes of local urban planners. The structure of power in China is such that local urban planners have no real authority over land-use control in their own cities if a ministry of the State Council has decided to establish a factory in a city. In industrial planning and factory location, it was not uncommon "to determine the factory site first, then find water later." (*Renmin ribao*, September 1, 1980, p. 1).

As indicated earlier, Beijing's industrial sector consumed 1.35 billion m^3 of water in 1978. It has been estimated that by the year 2000 this sector will need between 2 to 3 billion m^3 of water. The problem of insufficient water for industrial development in the city has been further complicated by declining water quality. Each day more than 1.8 million tons of untreated raw sewage are discharged into the city's streams, many of which have become nothing more than open sewers (*Renmin ribao*, June 16, 1980, p. 3).

The surface water network of Beijing consists of 46 rivers and ditches totaling 900 km in length. Except for the upper reaches of a few rivers that are still clean in distant suburbs, the other channels are polluted to varying degrees. More than 400 km of the network are affected by the discharge or dumping of industrial wastes, and 90 percent of the total stream length in the city proper and its immediate suburbs is polluted. At least 34 streams are seriously affected by industrial wastes and domestic sewage. Some of the streams emit offensive odors (*Renmin ribao*, September 12, 1980, p. 5).

As the city's population increases, more domestic sewage is produced. But the length of sewer lines and sewage treatment facilities has not been sufficiently expanded. In 1954, for example, the city had 600 km of sewers which carried 67,000 tons of sewage per day. In 1980 the amount of sewage was 29 times higher than that of 1954, while the length of sewer lines merely doubled. As a consequence, only 32 percent of the city's sewage could be carried by underground sewers, and the remainder must be discharged into streams, lakes, and ditches. Since the city now has only two sewage treatment plants (located at Gaobeidian and Jiuxianqiao, both in eastern suburbs), and only a few industries have their own treatment facilities, the streams are the only channels through which sewage is carried (*Renmin ribao*, September 12, 1980, p. 5). As the volumes and velocities of the stream water in Beijing are small and the quantity of sewage large, the streams' sewage loads are very heavy. In addition, as a result of the haphazard discharge of sewage, groundwater has been polluted in some localities. For example, four of the wells at the Seventh Water Company in the southern suburb of Beijing and 12 wells in the city have been rendered useless because of infiltration of toxic materials into the groundwater. Extensive areas of groundwater in Fangshan, a county in Greater Beijing, have been polluted by petrochemical factories to such an extent that to find safe drinking water has become a serious problem for many peasants (*Beijing ribao*, September 19, 1980, p. 3).

ENVIRONMENTAL POLICY AND THE PROTECTION OF WATER RESOURCES

The lack of a sufficient amount of surface water in Beijing is not the only factor that has contributed to water pollution. China's environmental policy, or the lack of it, plays an even more important role. To a large extent, the problems of Beijing's water are a result of the lack of effective environmental policies. Environmental issues were rarely discussed in China prior to the mid-1970s. Since then, more and more planners have been concerned about the danger of deteriorating environmental quality, and agencies of environmental protection have been established at the national and local levels. In 1979 an environmental law was adopted which provides general guidelines on environmental protection (*Annual Economic Report of China, 1981*, pp. II-157-159). In May 1980 the Secretariat of the Central Committee of the Chinese Communist Party issued a four-point "proposal" regarding Beijing's future development. Beijing must become

1. a model in public security, social order and moral standards for the whole country and one of the best in the world;
2. a first-rate modern city with a fine environment, high standards of cleanliness and good sanitation;
3. the nation's most developed city in culture, science and technology, with the highest educational standards in the country; and

4. a city with a thriving economy, providing its residents with stability in life and all kinds of conveniences. (*Beijing Review*, 1980, p. 15).

This directive, which in our opinion is sound and realistic, is important because it specifically calls for a better environment and points out that Beijing should be a political, cultural, research, and educational center rather than a major industrial base. Numerous articles appeared in the press shortly after the release of the directive, all in favor of curbing Beijing's heavy industrial sector from further expansion.

One basic problem of environmental protection confronting China's policymakers is how to monitor environmental quality and enforce environmental policies. While environmental standards exist in China, there are indications that many factories are unable to meet the standards because of inadequate facilities. It is not clear which agencies have been given the authority to enforce environmental laws and to take punitive actions against violators. Although the state requires that all new large-scale industries must include measures of environmental protection in their design, construction, and production, the lack of an administrative and legal apparatus that could effectively bring penalties to the polluting industries has hampered the progress of environmental work. Economic sanctions and fines appear to be unworkable because all of the large and medium-sized factories are state-owned. The state must ultimately bear all the monetary costs of penalty. Few leaders of the factories that are heavy polluters are known to have been dismissed or openly reprimanded, although a few polluting factories have been criticized publicly by the press. Meanwhile, the achievement of higher production quotas continues to be the major criterion used to judge the performance of industries. Factories producing more and better goods are seen as making a positive contribution to socialist industrialization, even though their waste materials heavily pollute the environment. Since most of the industries in Beijing are not new and lack anti-pollution facilities, it could take a long period of time before such facilities can be installed. Meanwhile, environmental degradation will continue in the foreseeable future.

SOME RECOMMENDATIONS

The problems of Beijing's water resources discussed in this paper must be dealt with immediately to ensure the quantity and quality of the city's future water supply. Water that is now available to Beijing must be used more efficiently and the question of water pollution must be addressed in a more effective manner. The achievement of these two goals is by no means easy and requires the successful interplay of a host of remedial measures. We feel the following recommended actions should be taken into consideration by proper authorities in any attempt to alleviate the existing problems of water:

1. A top-level administrative organ should be established in Beijing to coordinate the use of both surface and groundwater resources in a comprehensive and planned way. All water resources within Beijing belong to the city and no agency should be permitted to tap water freely without the prior consent of this coordinating organ. In coordinating the use of water, the needs of various interest groups as well as the directions of Beijing's future growth should be taken into consideration. It may be useful to establish stringent local legislations to regulate water use and to alleviate water pollution, all in the context of national environmental protection legislations.

2. More efficient use of industrial water has to be required. Since a large portion of urban Beijing's water is for industrial use, more industries should use water on a repetitive basis. Approximately 70 percent of the water used by industries is for cooling, and much of it should be cooled and reused. In Beijing the level of reuse is still low: only 20-30 percent of the industrial water is used again, and this could be raised to 60-70 percent to save approximately 400 million m^3 of water per year, an amount equal to some 40 percent of the water used by industries in Greater Beijing.

3. More efficient irrigation methods should be adopted to save agricultural water. In 1978 approximately 80 percent (5.1 million mu, or 340,000 hectares) of Beijing's farmland was irrigated, consuming 3 billion m^3 of water (Figure 2). A substantial amount of water could be saved by converting the existing surface irrigation method to sprinkling or drip irrigation methods. Generally speaking, the sprinkling method requires only 50 percent of the water used by surface irrigation, and drip irrigation needs only one-third to one-fourth the amount.

4. The waste water of Beijing should be treated and reused for irrigation, replacing the fresh water that is now being used for irrigation. This would make more water available for the city's

114

domestic sector. The quantities of water involved in such an exchange use are comparable.

5. Artificial recharge of groundwater should be carried out to raise the groundwater levels. In urban Beijing 98 percent of the domestic water used is supplied by groundwater. As a result of excessive tapping, deep cones of depression have been formed in an area of approximately 1,000 km^2 in and near urban Beijing. From 1971 to 1978, the overdraw of the city's groundwater amounted to almost 1.3 billion m^3, averaging 160 million m^3 per year. In addition to reducing the rate of pumping, a more positive way to alleviate the problem of groundwater shortage is by artificial recharge, which is feasible in many places in Beijing where the alluvial materials facilitate rapid infiltration of water. A significant amount of water could be channeled from the hilly regions to appropriate lowland localities during the flood season for artificial recharge. Among such localities are plain reservoirs, ancient river beds, and sand and gravel pits that have been abandoned. Experiments conducted in Beijing demonstrate that artificial recharge is effective, although more research is needed to solve a number of theoretical and actual problems (Brigade of Hydrogeology, 1980). Furthermore, artificial recharge not only enhances the supply of groundwater, it can also prevent land subsidence in Beijing.

6. A higher fee for water should be assessed. The cost of water is unreasonably low in China. Generally, it accounts for only 1 percent of the cost of industrial production (*Beijing ribao*, August 2, 1981, p. 4). As a consequence, few industries are concerned about saving water. In addition, most agencies and schools in Beijing subsidize their employees by paying for the bulk of the water used at home. On the average, each person pays only a token fee of 20 to 30 *fen* (about 12 to 18 cents) per month (*Renmin ribao*, August 12, 1981, p. 2). A recent investigation reveals that when residents are charged on the basis of the actual amount of water used, the level of consumption drops sharply. Water consumption in two adjacent apartment buildings located in the West District of Beijing was studied. The per capita consumption in the building where residents pay a flat fee was 8.5 tons for the month of April, 1981. In the other building, where water cost was assessed on the basis of actual amount used, the per capita consumption was only 2.4 tons for the same month (*Beijing wanbao*, June 7, 1981, p. 1). A large amount of domestic water could be saved in a city of 5 million urban residents if a higher fee is assessed.

7. Industries requiring a large quantity of water for operation, such as iron and steel, chemical, and power plants, must not be permitted to be constructed in and near urban Beijing, where there

is already a shortage of water. Construction of such industries must be prohibited especially in the upstream areas to the northwest of urban Beijing.

8. Stringent policies of enviromental monitoring must be developed and implemented to discourage environmental pollution. Officials in responsible positions in the factories and their superiors at higher levels must be held responsible for any actions they take that may result in environmental degradation. Among the penalties that should be considered for imposition on irresponsible officials are salary reduction, demotion, and dismissal from their positions.

9. Reforestation in the hilly regions in the northern and western parts of Beijing should be carried out to better regulate the movement of water, to prevent flooding, and to reduce water and soil erosion. In addition, more reservoirs should be built to provide more water. At present in Beijing there are 84 reservoirs which control about 60 percent of Beijing's hilly areas. The remaining 40 percent of the hilly regions have not been controlled, and approximately 2.3 billion m^3 of water per year could be utilized.

10. The population size of Beijing should be limited. As Figure 3 shows, the volume of domestic water consumption in the city has been increasing more rapidly than industrial water consumption. As the standards of living of the 5 million urban residents improve and as the city becomes more cosmopolitan, the demand for domestic water will continue to rise even without further population growth.

NOTE

1. The junior author would like to thank the Committee for Scholarly Communication with the People's Republic of China and the University of Akron for their support which enabled him to visit the U.S. in 1981-1982. The support made the preparation of this article possible.

LITERATURE CITED

Annual Economic Report of China, 1981 (Zhongguo jingji nianjian), 1981, Zhonghua renmin gongheguo huanjing baohufa (Environmental protection law of the People's Republic of China). Beijing: published by Journal of Economic Management (Jingji quanli zazhishe), pp. II-157-159.
Beijing Review, 1980, Building a new Beijing. *Beijing Review*, Vol. 23, No. 31, 14-16, 26.
Beijing ribao (Beijing Daily), 1980, (September 19), p. 3.

116

——— , , 1980, (October 17), p. 1.

——— , , 1981. (August 2), p. 2, 4.

——— , , 1981, (August 29), p. 1.

Beijing wanbao (Beijing Evening Press), 1981 (June 7), p. 1

Brigade of Hydrogeology and Engineering Geology, Beijing, and Station of Hydrogeology, Beijing, 1980, Dixiashui rengong huiguan shiyan yanjiu (Experimental research on artificial recharge of groundwater). *Shuiwen dizhi, gongcheng dizhi* (Hydrogeology and Engineering Geology), No. 1, p. 38.

Feng, Baoxing, Wan, Xin and Zhang, Dajian, 1980, Jiqu pianmian fazhan zhonggongye de lishi jiaoxun (Remember the historical lesson of one-sided development of heavy industry). *Xinhua yuebao* (*New China Monthly*), Abstracts Ed., No. 2, pp. 66–68.

Investigation Group of the Ministry of Water Resources, 1981, Beijingshi shuili jianshe xiaoyi diaocha (An investigation of the benefits and effects of water resources development in Beijing City). *Shuili jianshe* (Water Resources Development), No. 1, pp. 25–27.

Liu, Changming and Xie, Ming, 1981, *Beijing diqu shuiziyuan chubu diaocha* (A preliminary investigation of the water resources in the Beijing area). Unpublished research paper, Institute of Geography, Chinese Academy of Sciences, Beijing.

Ma, Laurence J.C., 1979, The Chinese approach to city planning: policy, administration, and action. *Asian Survey*, Vol. 19, No. 9, 838–855.

——— , , 1981, Urban housing supply in the People's Republic of China. In Laurence J.C. Ma and Edward W. Hanten, editors, *Urban Development in Modern China*. Boulder Colo.: Westview Press, pp. 222–259.

Renmin ribao (People's Daily), 1949, (March 17), p. 1.

——— , , 1980, (June 10), p. 2.

——— , , 1980, (June 16), p. 3.

——— , , 1980, (August 12), p. 2.

——— , , 1980, (September 1), p. 1, 3.

——— , , 1980, (September 12), p. 5.

——— , , 1981, (February 9), p. 2.

——— , , 1981, (August 12), p. 2.

Sha, Ying, 1980, Chengshi jianshe yao zunzhong kexue (Urban construction must respect science). *Chengshi jianshe* (*Urban Construction*), trial issue, November, pp. 6–9.

Zhu, Zuxi, 1980, Zong huanjing wuran de dianzhuang tan Beijing gongye de fazhan (A discussion on Beijing's industrial development on the basis of the present conditions of environmental pollution). *Huanjing baohu* (*Environmental Protection*), No. 5, pp. 5–7, 11, 35.

Nature Preserves and Protected Wildlife in the People's Republic of China[1]

Catherine S. Enderton

During the past decade the People's Republic of China has enlarged the scope of its environmental protection policy and has taken steps toward integrating the new policies into its national development plans. The new PRC Constitution stipulates that "The state ensures the rational use of natural resources and protects rare animals and plants" (*Beijing Review*, Dec. 27, 1982, p. 13). One facet of environmental protection involves nature preserves and the protection of endangered wildlife.

Nature preserves and protected wildlife are not the highest priority issues within the environmental protection policy of the PRC. Water conservancy; afforestation, reforestation, and forest protection; pollution control; pest control; birth planning; and other issues with greater immediate economic and health impact are considered more urgent matters. Yet new nature preserves have been established and more wildlife have been given the protection of the state in recent years.

Policy decisions in support of species conservation are an important step toward functional protection of endangered species. There is, however, still a considerable gap between China's articulated conservation policy and the implementation and enforcement of that policy. The main purpose of this paper is to

118

enumerate the PRC's stated policies, with regard to the protection of endangered plant and animal species and their habitats, and to describe the landscapes and populations at risk. The map supplement included here shows the 72 nature preserves and 54 species of protected wildlife in the People's Republic of China as of 1980. The text notes some of the additions to the list made between 1980 and 1982.

CHINA'S ENVIRONMENTAL POLICY

The Chinese have been involved in aspects of environmental protection since their civilization began. Edward H. Schafer chronicles one component of this as he writes of the emperors' support of "Hunting Parks and Animal Enclosures in Ancient China" (Schafer, 1968, pp. 318-343). Other features of China's long-standing environmental concerns are evident in centuries of highly effective intensive farming and water management techniques and repeated efforts at reforestation.

The PRC took an early interest in public health, forestry, and water conservancy. However, it was not until the 1972 Stockholm Conference on Human Environment that China adopted a full-scale, integrated environmental management policy.

Qu Geping and Li Jinchan of China's Office of Environmental Protection wrote in the United Nations' FAO publication *Unasylva*. In the publication they traced the history and development of the PRC's environmental policy from the Stockholm Conference to the present (Qu and Li, 1981, pp. 2-18). They explained that as a result of China's involvement in that international gathering, the PRC held its first national conference on environmental protection in 1973. In 1978 the new draft constitution was promulgated, and it included the state's explicit responsibility for protection of the environment. In 1979 environmental protection laws; forestry protection laws; aquatic resources protection laws; irrigation water standards laws; laws covering the quality of water for fishing; and laws on standards for safety in using insecticides were put forth in draft form. In 1980 China joined in signing the convention that controls international trade in endangered species of wild fauna and flora (Qu and Li, 1981, pp. 2-18).

The new environmental law offers some protection for the atmosphere, water, land, minerals, forests, grassland, wildlife, wild plants, aquatic life, historic sites, scenic spots for sightseeing, hot springs, health resorts, nature conservation areas, residential districts, natural environment, natural resources, and environment relating to living quarters (Qu and Li, 1981, p. 9).

A vice-premier of the state council heads the PRC's Leading Group for Environmental Protection. The Leading Group's members represent more than 20 departments including planning; construction; science; agriculture and forestry; industry; communications; health; education; oceanological research; and public security. The Office of the Leading Group has divisions of planning; science and technology; investigation and research; water resources; atmosphere; nature conservation; education; international liaison; and others. A research institute and a general monitoring station are being established. Environmental protection departments have been set up in the ministries of chemical industries; metallurgy; petroleum; light industry; textile industries; power; transportation and communications; railways; machine building; agriculture; forestry; public health; education and scientific research; and a research institute of oceanology under the state council (Qu and Li, 1981, p. 15).

Bureaus of environmental protection have been established in 22 provinces, autonomous regions, and municipalities. These bureaus are directed by the central government in Beijing. Those provinces that do not yet have a bureau of environmental protection have at least an office of environmental protection within an existing bureau or other provincial administrative unit. Most cities and counties also have environmental protection offices as do many large industrial and mining enterprises. The drainage regions of the Yangzi, Huang, and Songhua rivers and Bohai Bay and Guanting reservoirs have their own environmental protection offices as well (Qu and Li, 1981, p. 15). (The bureaus are a part of the vertical command structure and are accountable to higher-ranking units such as ministries; the offices of environmental protection are within bureaus or other units and are accountable horizontally to their unit.)

Qu and Li stated there are 15,000 persons working at China's environmental research institutes and monitoring stations (1981, p. 17). They discussed the administrative structure (in general, planning at the top and enforcement at the bottom) and cited the need for clarification and coordination in policy and enforcement, for more and better-trained personnel, and for more mass education to ensure the cooperation of all citizens.

Protection of flora and fauna is only a small part of the overall program, and its success depends on the effectiveness of nearly all the other aspects of environmental protection. Nevertheless, protection of endangered species appears to be included at every level of China's articulated environmental protection policy.

Inclusion of the difficult and possibly costly program of species protection is made the more noteworthy in view of some of the PRC's earlier attitudes toward environmental conservation, which stressed the priority of immediate economic benefit and the concept that nature was wasted when not utilized, tamed, and humanized (Boxer and Pramer, 1978, p. 7) (see also the many references in Salter, 1973). Public health improvement, pollution control, water conservancy, afforestation, and recycling have prompt economic return for the people of China, and have, as such, been the focus of most managerial concern. The formidable nature of the task of saving endangered species and their habitats becomes apparent when consideration is given to other factors including the pressure rural poverty is apt to exert on wildlife; the sensitivity nature conservation programs show to changing policy and political instability; and the considerable difficulties that ensue in China when cross-ministerial cooperation is needed. The importance of the long-term impact of environmental degradation was learned at Stockholm. Other explanations for China's new policies concerning nature preserves and protected species will be considered in the conclusion of the paper.

NATURE PRESERVES

There is no single comprehensive source that describes all the nature preserves of the PRC. One article by Liu Yukai of the Chinese Academy of Sciences Natural Resources Comprehensive Investigation Committee is the source of a list of the first 72 of the PRC's nature preserves that are shown on the map supplement (Liu, 1981, pp. 92–96). A similar, but not identical, list appeared in *Dongwuxue Zazhi* (*Chinese Journal of Zoology*) (Shi, 1981, pp. 41–45). *Zhonghua Renmin Gongheguo Dituji* (*National Atlas of the People's Republic of China*) (1979) describes some of the reserves in its text. My field notes from visits to several of the preserves during a nine-month stay in China, miscellaneous delegation trip reports, and items in the Chinese press provide more examples and indications of additional new developments.

Between 1956 and 1980 the PRC established 72 nature preserves in 21 provinces and autonomous regions with a total area equal to 0.17 percent of China's land area (Liu, 1981, p. 92). More than half

121

of these have been established since 1975, and 15 were established in 1980. Liu says that in accordance with the PRC policy of a

"comprehensive protection of natural environment, an enthusiastic promotion of scientific research, and a rational utilization of biological resources."

China should increase the number and variety of nature preserves and expand the areas to form a substantial national network (1981, p. 92). *Renmin ribao* cited a report of a national meeting on environmental protection at which it was suggested that the PRC government plans to increase the number of preserves to 300 to cover 1 percent of China's land area; "People's governments should carry out the plan as soon as possible and should regard it as a pressing and important task for our country" (October 22, 1980, p. 2). Discussion of a select few of these preserves will help to determine how "pressing and important" China perceives this aspect of environmental management.

The PRC's first nature preserve, Dinghu Mountain Preserve (#47 on the map supplement), was established in 1956. It lies astride the Tropic of Cancer, in the hills just north of the Xi Jiang (West River) and 110 km west of Guangzhou in China's southern Guangdong Province. Dinghu is the site of an ancient Buddhist temple, hence the locale of a traditionally protected forest. The total area of Dinghu Mountain Preserve is 1,000 ha of which 300 ha are 300-year-old subtropical monsoon evergreen forest (Author's field notes, 1980; Thorhaug, 1978, p. 52). The remaining 700 ha recently were replanted, mostly with Masson's Pine (*Pinus massoniana*). A listing of the 2,400 native plant species (278 families and 1,118 genera) of the preserve has been published. A number of trails have been developed in the preserve, and many local and Hong Kong tourists visit Dinghu Mountain. Botanists and ecologists from the Dinghu Mountain arboretum (a part of the Guangdong Provincial Institute of Botany) carry out research projects in the oldest native vegetation in an area that is off-limits to tourists.

In January 1980 Dinghu was one of three preserves to become part of the United Nations world biological protected areas network; the other two were Changbai Mountain Nature Preserve in Jilin Province in northeastern China, and Wolong Nature Preserve in northwestern Sichuan Province in central China. Because of this special international status of Dinghu, a number of foreign scientists have made research trips to the preserve.

China's southernmost nature preserve is Jianfengling (#53 on the map) on Guangdong's Hainan Island. Jianfengling includes 1,635 ha of protected forest centered on a mountain peak of 1,400 m. The mountaintop vegetation above 1,100 m consists of shrubs and mosses; from 600 to 1,100 m is tropical rain forest; from 300 to 600 m is seasonal rain forest; and below 300 m is scrub-covered hills and dry grassland. In 1949 the mountain was thought to have had about 25 percent coverage of old forest, but by 1979 the coverage had been reduced by lumbering and slash-and-burn agriculture to about 12 percent coverage of old forest and an additional 5 percent plantings of rubber trees. Today the remnant of old tropical rain forest is fully protected. Although the preserve was established in 1960, research did not begin there until 1974. Now the preserve has a staff of 150, of whom 80 are involved in research. There are six research offices: replanting; seeds and breeding; ecology; insect and disease control; timber utilization; and basic research.

Snakes and leeches were the only wildlife I actually saw in the preserve, but I was told that rare deer (including a species of locally-called Dongfang deer, of which there are reportedly only 20 in existence), monkeys, and birds still inhabit the forest.

Zhalong Nature Preserve (#5) in Heilongjiang is the largest bird preserve in China. It is located southeast of Qiqihar City. The preserve is home to more than 100 species of fowl, including many crane species. The most famous crane in the preserve is the red-headed crane (*Grus japonensis*). Much of the land surrounding the preserve was a marsh reclaimed by retired armymen and organized into state farms (*Zhonghua Renmin Gongheguo Dituji*, 1979, text to map 39).

Changbai Mountain Nature Preserve in Jilin (#6) is located along the border with North Korea. It is one of the largest preserves and is rich in environments, plants, and wildlife. Volcanic lakes, waterfalls, and hot springs characterize the habitat for more than 1,400 plant species (including more than 700 medicinal plants, pines, and firs) and for rare animals (including tigers, leopards, and musk deer).

Shedao (Snake Island) Preserve (#7) in Liaoning Province is also called Xiaolongshan (Small Dragon Mountain). It is a small island offshore from Luda City (Darien). The island has an abundance of caves and fractures in the rocks that provide an excellent environment for poisonous sea snakes. Some of the many snakes that thrive there are used for medicinal purposes.

Niaodao (Bird Island) Preserve is located in the northwest corner of Qinghai Lake in Qinghai Province. The preserve is the summer home to 100,000 migratory birds. The saline lake's deep blue waters are said to teem with fish, including a sturgeon that the birds eat. Visitors are not admitted to the preserve without passes, and no

123

visitors are allowed during breeding season. Geese, cormorants, seagulls, and white swans nest here in May, and hatchlings are everywhere in June. In September the flocks head south (Ye, 1982, p. 10).

There are 13 nature preserves in Sichuan Province. The most famous one is Wolong (#26) in Wenchuan County. It is the major home of the greatly endangered giant panda.

Huaping Preserve (#57) in Guangxi Province is noted for its ancient silver pines (*Cathaya argyrothylla*). Shennongjia Preserve (#20) in forested mountainous western Hubei Province is especially known for its medicinal herbs. It is supposed to be the place where the god of agriculture built his drying rack in order to taste all herbs.

For many of the nature preserves listed in the table on the back of the map supplement, no additional information was available. Tibet, Hebei, Shandong, and Jiangsu do not yet have nature preserves. The series of articles that has recently appeared in the Chinese press introducing readers to various nature preserves and protected species of rare wildlife, may herald the establishment of new preserves.

In fact, *Beijing Review* says that as of April 1982, there was a total of 85 preserves established (April 5, 1982, p. 28). Some of the new preserves which do not appear on the map supplement include Kanas Lake and Altai Mountain preserves in Xinjiang, where "a vast stretch of rolling pastureland, nourished by rivers and lakes, surrounds the Friendship Peak located in China's far north-western corner" (*China Pictorial*, No. 3, 1982, p. 30). It covers 300,000 ha and the flora consists of European aspen, Siberian juniper, fir, and spruce as well as shrubs, grasses, and aquatic plants. There are more than 100 species of wild animals including the wolverine, red deer, snow leopard, snow hare, sable, grouse, and ptarmigan. The preserve "is only frequented by a few herdsmen who are occasionally joined by scientists" (*China Pictorial*, No. 3, 1982, p. 30).

Another preserve, which was established in 1980 and which does not appear on the map supplement, is Mengda Nature Preserve in Xunhua Sala Autonomous County in Qinghai. It has an area of 10,000 ha and was established mainly to protect rare tree species. Two of Heilongjiang's new preserves are Jingpo Lake Nature Preserve with an area of 154,000 ha in Ningan County and Qising Lizi Nature Preserve in Guanang and Ji counties. The Qising Lizi Nature Preserve covers 33,000 ha and is a habitat for the Siberian tiger. Guangdong also has several new preserves, among them is

124

Qingpi Forest Nature Preserve with 1,066 ha in Hainan's Nanning County, and Heishiding Nature Preserve with 1,333 ha of semitropical rain forest in Fengkai County. Study of these preserves and their associated species should point Chinese and Western scientists to appropriate field sites for the study of China's rare and precious species.

PROTECTED WILDLIFE

Geographers of the Chinese Academy of Sciences in their monograph, *Dongwu Dili* (*Animal Geography*, which is part of the series *China's Natural Geography*), discuss the "control and utilization" of China's wildlife (*Dongwu Dili*, 1979, pp. 114-116). Their discussion proceeds according to seven zoogeographical regions, which are outlined below. (See Figure 1 and Table 1.) As noted on the map supplement, those animals protected by the state are subject to three levels of protection: "hunting controlled," "hunting strictly controlled," and "hunting forbidden."

TABLE 1

ENDANGERED AND PROTECTED WILDLIFE BY ZOOGEOGRAPHIC REGION

Region I Northeast China	Region II North China	Region III Mongolia & Xinjiang	Region IV Qinghai & Tibet	Region V Southwest China	Region VI Central China	Region VII South China
Swan	Giant salamandar	Whooper swan	Tibetan eared pheasant	Black-necked crane	Giant salamander	Long-tailed pheasant
Mandarin duck	Brown eared pheasant	Pheasants	Brown eared pheasant	Rhesus macaque	Crocodile lizard	Bambo pheasant
Red-headed crane	Long-tailed pheasant	Quail	Tibetan snowcock	Golden langur	Yangtze alligator	Green peafowl
White-headed crane	Japanese crested ibis	Tibetan snowcock	Tibetan snowcock	Lesser panda	Swan	Great pied hornbill
Great white crane	Rhesus macaque	Great bustard	Black necked crane	Marten	Mandarin ducks	Malabar pied hornbill
Wolf	Snow rabbit	Marmot	Quail	Golden cat	Cranes	Loris
Weasel	Flying squirrel	Mongolian beaver	Himalayan brown bear	Clouded leopard	Rehesus macaque	Taiwan macaque
Sable	Wolf	Weasel	Snow leopard	Snow leopard	Golden langurs	Pig-tailed macaque
Wolverine	Weasel	Marten	Wild donkey	Rhinoceros	Yangtze dolphins	White-headed langur
Badger	Sable	Badger	White-lipped deer	White-lipped deer	Giant Panda	Golden langur
Siberian tiger	Stone marten	Lynx	Sika deer	Sika deer	Yellow weasel	Gibbon
Leopard	Lynx	Przewalski's horse	Tibetan antelope	Horse deer	Hog badger	Chinese pangolin
Amur leopard	Musk deer	Wild donkey	Yak	River deer	Ferret badger	Civet
Musk deer	Sika deer	Bactrian camel	Rock sheep	Takin	Yellow skunk	Masked palm civet
Sika deer	Pere David's deer	Hillier's gazelle	Big horn sheep	Golden takin	South China tiger	Golden cat
Moose	Horse deer	Mongolian gazelle			Sika deer	South China tiger
Reindeer	Roe deer	Tibetan antelope			Musk deer	Clouded leopard
Mongolian gazelle	Mongolian gazelle	Saiga antelope			Black muntjac deer	Hainan slope deer
Goral	Goral	Goral			River deer	Sika deer
		Big horn sheep			Goral	River deer
					Serow	Gaur

Source: Compiled by author.

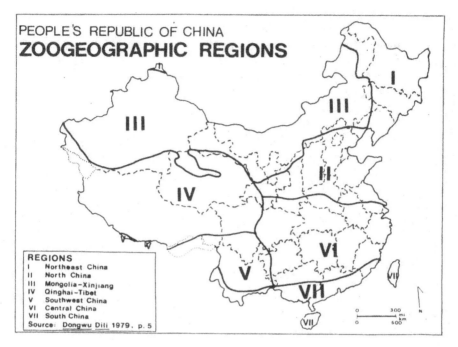

Figure 1

Region I: The Northeast

The Northeast (Dongbei) zoogeographical region includes the northeastern tip of Inner Mongolia, Heilongjiang, Jilin, eastern Liaoning, and the northern tip of Xinjiang. It is considered by Chinese biogeographers to be an area rich in wildlife due to the extensive stands of old coniferous forest. It is China's principal fur-trapping area. Game hunting is also important there. Squirrel, weasel, deer, boar, and pheasant are the most often sought fauna.

Rare species in the Northeast zoogeographic region include the Siberian tiger, moose, reindeer, sika deer, musk deer, goral, wolverine (*Gulo gulo*), red-headed crane, great white crane, white-headed crane, two species of swan, and the Mandarin duck. (See the table on the back of the map supplement for more taxonomy.) The great white crane may now be extinct (*Renmin ribao*, October 22, 1980).

126

The Siberian tiger receives the maximum protection of the law. According to a recent article, since 1949, 128 Siberian tigers have been hunted down and killed (38 in the area of the Mudan river, 10 near the Songhua River, 31 near the He River, 35 near Yinchuan City, and 14 in other places) (*Dili Zhishi*, July 1981, p. 12). Not only has their distribution been shrinking rapidly, but the tigers were becoming so widely scattered and isolated from one another that they were further endangered by the difficulty of finding mates during the breeding season. Since the issuance of the laws on hunting and forestry, two preserves have been established in Heilongjiang to preserve the tiger. The two preserves were both established in 1980. One is Qixing (Seven Star) Preserve covering 33,000 ha and located in eastern Heilongjiang; and the other is Jingpuo (Mirror Lake) Preserve consisting of 154,000 ha. Seven Star Preserve now reports 19 tigers in the area, and Mirror Lake Preserve reports 10 tigers. Another tiger preserve is the Changbai nature preserve in Jilin Province, but it is not known how many animals exist there (Swannack-Nunn, Bowman, and Heffernan, 1979, p. 273). The Chinese estimate that the total count of tigers in the wild (including the preserves) is approximately 80.

A *Renmin ribao* article on recently extinct animals included "the Xinjiang Tiger" (October 22, 1980). The reference is possibly to the Siberian tigers in northernmost Xinjiang or possibly to Amur leopards (*Panthera pardus orientalis*) in that same area. The UNEP was informed that the Amur leopard is extremely rare and that hunting it is forbidden, but that no preserve has been established for it. They also report that leopard skins and leopard skin coats (at 2,100 yuan each) were on sale in fur shops they visited. The UNEP personnel think most of these were probably from the more common leopard, *Panthera pardus japonensis* since the two subspecies are difficult to tell apart (Swannack-Nunn et al., 1979, p. 274).

Five species of deer are protected in the Northeast Region. Hunting the musk deer (*Moschus moschiferus*) is strictly regulated. Its glands secrete an oil valuable to the perfume industry. The Chinese have recently devised a way to extract the musk from the live deer. They are also experimenting with deer farms. According to the UNEP, five or six farms have been set up with several dozen deer on each farm, but the musk produced so far is quite insufficient to meet the needs and demand of the PRC. The musk thus produced is not available for export (Swannack-Nunn et al., 1979, p. 278). The UNEP feels that wild musk deer poaching will continue to be a problem for the foreseeable future because the discrepancy between supply and demand for musk is growing.

127

The sika deer (*Cervus nippon* spp.) also receive the second level of protection. Hunting of moose and reindeer is regulated, as is hunting the Mongolian gazelle (*Procapra gutturosa gutturosa* and *P.g. altaica*).

Four small fur-bearing carnivores are listed as objects of protection in Region I. The weasel (*Mustela sibrica*) and the sable (*Martes zibellina*) receive the minimum level of protection. The wolverine is also protected. Hunting regulations cover the badger (*Meles meles leptorynchus*), which is found in both Heilongjiang and the northern tip of Xinjiang. In these damp areas of China, this little animal has been an important resource. Its thick hide is useful because it is nearly waterproof. Badger hides were made into rugs and spread on brick kangs (sleeping platforms) or in carts (Allen, 1938, p. 58). Sowerby writes, "Manchurian hunters all wear nicely dressed badger skins hanging from their belts at the back, in which position they are always ready to form a dry seat" (Sowerby, 1914, p. 48).

Protected birds in Region I include swans and Mandarin ducks (*Aix galericulata*) which are China's love birds and are always shown in pairs. They are often chosen as the decoration for wedding gifts. Both swans and Mandarin ducks can be hunted only under strict regulation. Hunting is also strictly regulated for the large red-headed crane (*Grus japonensis*). The red-headed crane winters along the lower reaches of the Chang Jiang and in Taiwan. In the spring it migrates to Heilongjiang where it breeds and raises its young. The Zhalong Nature Preserve (#5 on the map supplement) has been designated as a crane reserve. Cheng Tso-hsin, in his 1964 book on China's economic birds, explains that the crane is an important symbol to the Chinese because it has a life span of 50-60 years and is often associated with pine trees. The crane is used as a longevity symbol, and there is the saying, "long life with pine and crane." Cheng says that the cranes need protection because the peasants of Dongbei hunt them for eggs and meat and sell their feathers and skins for export to foreign markets (Cheng, 1964, p. 236). *Beijing Review* reports that in 1981 for the first time a few eggs of the red-headed crane were successfully hatched in an incubator (April 5, 1982, p. 28). Another crane, the Great White or Siberian Crane (*Grus leucogeranus*) may now be extinct, according to *Renmin ribao* (Oct. 22, 1980, p. 2). The UNEP reports that although these cranes have not been sighted for some time, a full investigation into their status has not been done (Swannack-Nunn et al., 1979, p. 279). Since five of China's eight species of crane (including four of the five endangered species) winter along the lower reaches of the Chang

128

Jiang (Yangtze River), the UNEP suggests that refuge areas be established there for them.

Region II: North China

The North China Region includes most of Hebei, all of Shanxi and Shandong, most of Shaanxi and Ningxia, and northern Jiangsu, Anhui, and Henan. This heavily populated region of China has little remaining forest or large wildlife. Chinese environmental geographers contend that reforestation will increase the population of such valuable wildlife as the Mongolian gazelle, musk deer, Pere David's deer (red deer), weasel, sable, snow rabbit, and lynx. Pheasants and rabbits are already said to be more abundant for hunting. Their population recovered after the conclusion of the Sino-Japanese and Chinese Civil Wars. The end of the wars allowed progress in reforestation. In the northern part of the loess plateau Roe-deer (*Capreolus capreolus*) are hunted under management regulations. The number of deer present and the level of hunting protection are, however, unspecified.

Protected species in the North China Region include the giant salamander (*Andrias davidianus*), for which hunting is regulated. Hunting of the brown eared pheasant is strictly regulated, as is that of the white-crowned, long-tailed pheasant (*Syrmaticus ellioti*). None of the North China wildlife currently falls in the total protection category of forbidden hunting with the possible exception of the recently rediscovered Japanese ibises (*Nipponia nippon*) (*Beijing Review*, April 5, 1982, pp. 28–29).

Protected mammals of north China include the rhesus macaque monkey (hunting regulated), the stone marten or muskrat (hunting regulated), and the musk deer and sika deer (both strictly regulated).

North China sika deer (*Cervus nippon mandarinus*) are valued for their antlers, which are an important component of Chinese traditional medicine. The antlers are collected while still in the velvet. Chinese authorities told the UNEP delegation that the numbers of north China sika in the wild are low, and a reevaluation of their protection status is in progress (Swannack-Nunn et al., 1979, p. 276). They said that there is a nature preserve set aside for them in Jilin. This may be the Changbai Mountain Nature Preserve (#6). North China sika are being bred extensively on deer farms. However, the UNEP warns that unless careful measures are taken to identify and segregate the various breeding stocks, there is danger of losing the subspecies through interbreeding among the several taxa. Other subspecies of sika include the Shanxi sika (*Cervus nippon grassianus*), the recently discovered Sichuan sika (*Cervus nippon szechwanensis*), and the South China sika (*C.n. koapschi*). The Shanxi sika are reported to be highly endangered, but there is as yet no nature preserve set aside for them. After querying people in and around the Dazhai Commune in central western Shanxi, and Ling Xian on the borders of Shanxi and Henan (site of the Red Flag Canal), the UNEP delegation came to the conclusion that it is likely that the Shanxi sika is extinct. They conclude their summary notes on China's endangered deer by commenting that:

> No country in the world possesses as many species of deer as does China. It is imperative, therefore, that from the commercial point of view as well as of course from the point of view of nature conservation and preservation of genetic resources, that special attention should be given to the protection of deer species in the wild which ipso facto implies the conservation of their habitat
>
> (Swannack-Nunn et al., 1979, p. 281).

Another animal for which hunting is regulated is the goral of the North China Region. The goral is a goat-like bovid and also is called the Himalayan chamois.

Three more mammals have been cited by the Chinese geographers as being in need of protection but are currently unregulated. These are the horse deer (*Cervus elaphus*) and two flying squirrels, the groove-toothed or Chinese flying squirrel (*Aeretes melanopterus*) and the complex-toothed flying squirrel (*Trogopterus xanthipes*).

The northwestern frontier of the North China Region has had a serious problem with excess rodent populations, especially the rock squirrel (*Sciurotamias davidianus* and *S. forresti*) and two rats, the yellow rat (*Ratus losea*) and the spotted rat (taxonomy unknown). The problem is said to be "basically under control" but in need of continuing vigilance (*Dongwu Dili*, 1979, p. 116).

The wolf (*Canis lupus*) is mentioned by the Chinese as a threat to deer herds. The UNEP delegation was told that a few stray wolves have recently been seen in the Taihang Mountains in southwestern Shanxi (Swannack-Nunn et al., 1979, p. 273). Wolves do not receive the protection of the state.

130

Region III: Mongolia and Xinjiang

The Mongolian and Xinjiang Region includes most of Nei Monggol and Xinjiang and parts of Qinghai, Ningxia, and Shaanxi. It consists predominantly of deserts and grasslands, where antelope, gazelle, quail, and pheasant are the main game hunted. Martens, weasels, badgers, gorals, and bighorn sheep are also hunted, but they are not abundant. So their hunting is restricted. Feathers, hides, and furs are marketed.

Specific species that fall under protection regulations include several large fowl, such as the whooper swan (hunting strictly regulated), the great bustard (*Otis tarda tarda*) (hunting regulated), and the Tibetan snowcock (*Tetragallus tibetanus*) (hunting regulated). Two rodents are trapped for their pelts, the Mongolian beaver (*Castor fiber*) (hunting regulated) and the marmot, also called the woodchuck or groundhog (*Marmota* spp.). Marmot hunting is not restricted because the Chinese worry that the marmot will become a pest if its numbers are allowed to increase. Protected at the least restricted level are two small fur-bearing carnivores, the stone marten (*Martes foina*) and the weasel. The lynx is also hunted; apparently it is not yet specifically protected, but the geographers recommend it for protection (*Dongwu Dili*, 1979, p. 116).

Two highly endangered animals in the Mongolian-Xinjiang Region are in the forbidden hunting category, Przewalski's horse (sometimes called the wild Mongolian pony) and the Bactrian camel. In fact, both now may be extinct in the wild. *Renmin ribao* (October 22, 1980) listed Przewalski's horse among 10 Chinese birds and animals recently declared extinct in the wild. (A number of these primitive horses survive in zoos). The UNEP delegation to China was told that a small group of the wild horses was recently reported sighted, and an expedition is being planned to search for the relics of the population. If the Chinese find Mongolian ponies surviving, a nature preserve will be set up to protect them (Swannack-Nunn et al., 1979, p. 274).

Hunting the wild donkey is strictly regulated. Conservationists are worried about its shrinking population and have suggested it also be considered for the full protection category.

Hillier's gazelle (*Gazelle subgutturosa*) and the Mongolian gazelle are included in the regulated-hunting category, but hunting the rare Tibetan antelope (*Pantholaps hodgsoni*) is forbidden. The Tibetan antelope was held sacred by the Mongols and the Tibetan Tangut tribe, who thought highly of the medicinal value of its blood and used the rings on its horns to predict the future. The Tibetan antelope may have been the basis for stories of the unicorn. When viewed from the side and at a distance, the Tibetan antelope's two long horns look like one horn (Walker, 1964, p. 1464).

Another animal that it is forbidden to hunt is the odd-looking saiga antelope (*Saiga tatarica* and *S.t. mongolica*). In prehistoric times the range of the saiga antelope extended from Poland to Mongolia. The vast herds provided Neolithic hunters with the bulk of their game. Saiga meat is said to be tender and tasty, and it continues to be popular game in modern times. These hearty migratory bovids experience dramatic population peaks and crashes according to climatic conditions in their Inner-Asian winter range. They are superb range animals for arid regions because they can endure for long periods without water and can eat highly saline vegetation. But they are sensitive to extreme cold; vast numbers can die during record temperature lows. To add to their troubles, their horns are prized ingredients in Chinese traditional medicine. A pair of saiga horns can bring U.S. $250, a small fortune to a peasant (Walker, 1964, p. 1465). Due to increased hunting and competition from herds of domestic cattle for their range, there were barely 200 individual saiga antelope left by 1920. Now they are strictly protected, especially by the Soviet Union, and their numbers have recovered to more than a million. However, their range is a mere fraction of its former expanse.

The subspecies (*Saiga tatarica mongolica*) has not fared so well. The UNEP delegation was told that the subspecies is very rare. The *Renmin ribao* (Oct. 22, 1980, p. 2) article on recently extinct animals listed the "high-nosed antelope" which may refer to this subspecies of saiga.

The Mongolia-Xinjiang Region has two more protected bovids, the goral and the bighorn sheep (*Ovis ammon darvini*). Their hunting is regulated.

Region IV: Qinghai and Tibet

In the remote and rugged terrain of Tibet and Qinghai, there is comparatively less human pressure on wildlife than there is in the heavily populated regions of eastern and southern China. Hunting, however, has brought a number of species to dangerously low levels of population. The most frequently hunted species are the bighorn sheep, rock sheep (*Pseudois nayaur*) and game birds such as quail and pheasants.

132

Protected birds include the very rare black-necked crane (*Grus nigricollis*). The UNEP delegation saw one specimen in the Shanghai Zoo, but they were not able to get information on its status in the wild beyond the fact that it is the rarest of China's eight species of crane. *Beijing Review* mentions a rare "black-collared crane" that summers in the lakes of the Qinghai-Tibet Plateau and winters in Yunnan and western Guizhou Provinces (April 5, 1982, p. 28). This may be the same crane.

China has the largest number of pheasant species of any country. Most are not considered endangered, but several of those in Region IV are protected; the Tibetan eared pheasant (*Crossoptilon crossoptilon*) and the brown eared pheasant (*C. mantchuricum*) fall in the category for strictly regulated hunting. The Tibetan snowcock and the Tragopan pheasant (*Tragopan* ssp.) are in the regulated-hunting group.

Plateau tribesmen have long respected and conserved waterfowl, consequently there are numbers of them surviving in Region IV. One of China's famous nature preserves, Bird Island (Niaodao) on Qinghai Lake, is summer home to 650 different kinds of waterfowl (half of all the varieties native to China) (*China Reconstructs*, July 1982, pp. 10–13).

Little information is available on the status and range of the snow leopard (*Panthera uncia*). According to the UNEP report, it is not believed to be gravely endangered; however, its numbers are thought to be quite low in some parts of its formerly wide range throughout the highlands of Central Asia (Swannack-Nunn et al., 1979, p. 274). On the books, hunting the magnificent snow leopard is strictly regulated. Yet, in the summer of 1981, Orville Schell traveled to Mount Anyemaquen, the homeland of the Golok tribesmen of Qinghai Province, where he witnessed his Golok guides hunt and shoot a snow leopard. Schell photographed a sign on a local state-run store offering to buy snow leopard bones, Himalayan brown bear livers, and white-lipped deer antlers for use in traditional Chinese medicine. The Golok hunters told him that the leopard bones should bring them 100 yuan (U.S. $60) (Schell, 1982, pp. 48–57).

The wild yak (*Bos grunniens mutus*) is found in isolated high mountains widely distributed throughout the Qinghai-Tibet Plateau. In early winter, according to the *Beijing Review*, some yaks cross into Kashmir (November 23, 1981, p. 30). The UNEP report says that although wild yaks often interbreed with domestic yaks, there is little hunting pressure on them, and there seems to be no problem involved in protecting them at the minimum level. Wild donkey hunting is strictly regulated. The rock sheep and bighorn sheep fall in the regulated hunting group.

Among the many deer in Region IV, the white-lipped deer (*Cervus albirostris*) is considered especially endangered. Its antlers in velvet are coveted for medicinal use. It is fully protected, and hunting it is forbidden. The Tibetan antelope is also fully protected in the Qinghai-Tibet Region, as it is in Xinjiang. The sika deer and musk deer also receive the same strictly regulated hunting protection that they are accorded elsewhere in China.

Region V: Southwest China

The Southwest China Region includes most of Yunnan, southern Sichuan, and a small part of southern Tibet. It is smaller in extent than Regions III or IV, but has an equally rugged and forested terrain and great diversity in wildlife. The southwest China region has a long list of "rare and precious" wildlife. The black-necked crane and several other rare fowl are found here.

Among Southwest China's protected mammals are listed the snow leopard and the clouded leopard (*Neofelis nebulosa*). Another protected wildcat is the golden cat (*Felis temmincki*). There are thought to be a few elephants and rhinoceros surviving in remote areas along the Burma border.

Several protected monkeys are listed in the Chinese sources. The common rhesus macaque (*Macaca mulatta*) is protected at the minimum level of hunting regulation. The rare golden langur (*Rhinopithecus roxellanae*) is fully protected. In ancient China princes and high-ranking officials treasured coats made of langur pelts. Today langurs are found in Sichuan, Gansu, Shaanxi, and western Hubei's Dashennongjia area.

Other small protected mammals include the stone marten and the lesser panda (*Ailurus fulgens*). This raccoon-like creature looks nothing like the giant panda. Hunting the lesser panda is strictly controlled.

The takin, which looks like a large goat, is a fully protected animal. According to the UNEP, there are two subspecies, *Budorcas taxicolor tibetana* and the golden takin, *B.t. bedfordi*. The former has been seen in herds of 300–400 animals and is not considered in danger of extinction. The golden takin is found only on the Great White Mountain of the Qinling range in southern Shanxi province, and little is known about its status. Sika deer, white-lipped deer,

134

river deer (*Hydropotes inermis*), and horse deer are also protected in southwestern China.

Region VI: Central China

The Central China Region includes southernmost Gansu and Shaanxi, western Henan, Hubei, and Hunan, northern Guangxi, most of Guizhou, and eastern Sichuan. This large region includes much of the Sichuan plain and the valley of the Chang Jiang, two of the most heavily populated parts of China. It is also the region with the largest number of nature preserves, although many of them are small.

The Chinese biogeographers listed the following "abundant wildlife" in Region VI: the yellow skunk, yellow weasel, ferret badger, hog badger, old world badger, civet, masked palm civet, raccoon dog, fox, and crab-eating mongoose. Apparently none of these small mammals are protected, nor do the geographers suggest they are in need of protection.

There is one protected amphibian and two protected reptiles in Region VI: the giant salamander, the crocodile lizard (*Shinisaurus crocodilurus*), and the Yangtze alligator (*Alligator sinensis*). Seven hundred years ago, at the time of Marco Polo's trip, Yangtze alligators were plentiful and were hunted for food in both southern and eastern China. As recently as the early 1950s loud, vibrant alligator roars were heard at night in Anhui Province, but today they are rarely heard, and alligator eggs are discovered only occasionally. However, they are not yet extinct. An alligator farm has been established in Xuancheng County, Anhui, which boasts more than 100 alligators (*China Pictorial*, March 1982, pp. 6–9).

The Central China rare and protected bird species include cranes, swans, and Mandarin ducks that winter along the lower reaches of the Yangtze. In the waters of the lower Chang Jiang (Yangtze) there are still some Yangtze River dolphins (*Lipotes vixillifer*). According to the UNEP delegation, there are very few dolphins left. Although they are not eaten, they are used for oil and are often trapped in fishing nets. The forested mountains of Region VI are said to have some rhesus macaques and golden langurs as well as the clouded leopard and the South China tiger (*Panthera tigris amuresis*), which is fully protected.

Most famous of all the protected species of Central China is the giant panda (*Ailuropoda melanoleuca*). Chinese experts estimate today's total panda population is less than 1,000. The prehistoric range of the giant panda, from Xi'an to Guangzhou and Burma to Wuhan, has shrunk to six small discontinuous areas from Xi'an south through Sichuan (Schaller, 1981, p. 735). In 1975 and 1976 the deaths of 138 giant pandas in areas bordering Sichuan and Gansu were traced to the widespread deterioration of the bamboo groves that provide their main source of food. Giant pandas propagate very slowly in the wild and only very occasionally in captivity. The combination of their limited numbers, discontinuous range, and the threat of starvation from the periodic widespread dying of bamboo, led China to establish a panda research institute. China has been inviting international scientists to join Chinese scientists in an effort to save the species. The World Wildlife Fund, for which the symbol is the panda, has been invited to do a joint field study in Sichuan's Wolong Nature Preserve (Schaller, 1981, pp. 735–749). The Chinese report that since 1978, 16 giant panda cubs have been born to zoos in Beijing, Chengdu, Hangzhou, and Shanghai. Five of the cubs are still alive, and three of these are more than three years old. China has exported 39 giant pandas since 1937. Fourteen of them are still living.

Central China is home to five protected deer species: the sika deer, the river deer, the musk deer, the tufted deer, and the rare black muntjac deer (*Muntiacus crinifrons*). Two bovids, the goral and the serow (*Capricornis sumatraensis*), are also protected.

Region VII: South China

The South China Region includes southern Fujian, most of Guangdong with all of Hainan Island, southern Yunnan, and Taiwan. Although Taiwan no doubt has its own wildlife protection regulations and list of endangered species, the ones listed here are those Beijing has designated as protected species. South China also includes China's tropics, her third longest river (the Xi Jiang), a major center of population (the Pearl River delta), and a number of forested mountains and nature preserves.

The southwest corner of Region VII borders on Burma. The remote jungles of this border still shelter wild Asiatic elephants; however, a *Renmin ribao* (Oct. 22, 1980, p. 2) article on recently extinct animals includes the elephant in the list of animals on the verge of extinction. The same area is home to the gaur (wild cattle) (*Bos gaurus*), the South China tiger, the clouded leopard, and the golden cat.

136

South China is the natural habitat for more than half a dozen endangered primates including the loris (*Nycticebus coucang*), the golden langur, the gibbon (*Hylobates concolor*), the Taiwan macaque (*Macaca cyclopis*), the pig-tailed macaque (*Macaca nemestrina*), and the extremely rare leaf monkey or white-headed langur (*Presbytis leucocephalus*). The white-headed langurs live only in the southern part of Guangxi and are thought to number approximately 600 individuals (*Beijing Review*, November 23, 1981, p. 30). These animals are sheltered by hunting restrictions.

In January 1982 the *Beijing Review* reported that 1,000 macaques had been discovered on four islands off the mouth of the Pearl River in Guangdong Province. The small islands (called Neilingding, Shangchuan, Dangan, and Erzhou) have been proposed as a nature preserve (January 25, 1982, p. 30).

Three small mammals are mentioned by Chinese biogeographers as protected or in need of protection in South China. They are the civet, the masked palm civet, and the Chinese pangolin (scaly anteater) (*Manis pentadactyla*). The pangolin is frequently trapped by peasants and sold as a food delicacy. I saw several live ones for sale in rural markets and one in front of the train station in Guangzhou. A Harvard Museum of Comparative Zoology associate who traveled briefly in South China reported being offered a meal of pangolin in a restaurant. He chose instead a meal of a five-pound bamboo rat (Lazell, 1982, pp. 52–56).

South China deer include the sika deer, river deer, hog deer (*Axis porcinus*), and the Hainan slope deer (*Cervus eldi siamensis*). The Hainan slope deer has been listed in the *Renmin ribao* as being on the verge of extinction. It is fully protected. The status of the hog deer is not known.

Endangered and protected birds of South China include the green peafowl (*Pavo muticus*) and the great pied hornbill (*Buceros bicornis*). Both are in the hunting regulated category. Mention is also made of the Malabar and pied hornbill (*Anthracoceros coronatus*) but its status is not stated. The long-tailed pheasant is both on the mainland and on Taiwan. Another Taiwanese bird that is mentioned is the Taiwan blue pheasant (*Lophura swinhoii*). Its status is not given. Mentioned as in need of protection is the bamboo pheasant (*Bambusicola thoracica*).

MAP SUPPLEMENT: DISTRIBUTION MAP OF CHINA'S NATURE PRESERVES AND PROTECTED WILDLIFE

The map supplement showing the nature preserves and protected wildlife in the People's Republic of China is printed at the scale of 1:10,000,000. The 1979 CIA map,"China," is also of the same scale and projection and can be used as an underlay on a light table in order to combine physical and political information with the distribution of nature preserves and protected wildlife. Pinyin spelling is used for Chinese names.

The information on this map supplement is based primarily on two Chinese sources. The first is the book, *Dongwu Dili (Animal Geography)*, edited in 1979 by the Chinese Academy of Sciences as a part of their series on the natural geography of China and published in Beijing. Maps in this volume, especially the supplemental map, "The Distribution of China's Rare and Precious Animals," provided the general location for the animals shown on my map.

The second source was an article in the Chinese journal *Ziran Ziyuan (Natural Resources)*, Volume 2, 1981, "The present nature preserves in China and their distribution," by Liu Yukai of the Chinese Academy of Sciences Comprehensive Investigation Committee on Natural Resources. This article provided the latitude and longitude for each of the 72 nature preserves listed. The list includes those preserves established up to early 1980.

Tables of the nature preserves and protected wildlife appear on the reverse side of the map supplement. Bird taxonomy follows that in James F. Clements' *Birds of the World: A Check List* (1978). Mammal taxonomy for genera and species follows that in Ernest P. Walker's *Mammals of the World* (1964). Subspecies designations are those given in the Chinese sources.

A word on accuracy and interpretation is in order. The distribution of nature preserves is based on latitudes and longitudes provided in the Liu article; however, the total area of all the nature preserves indicated on the map is only 0.17 percent of China's land area. Therefore, the symbols for nature preserves are considerably larger than they would be if they were shown to scale. The animal symbols indicate approximate ranges of the animals.

Only tentative inferences concerning wildlife in specific preserves can be made from the geographic proximity of animals and preserves as illustrated on the map.

138

CONCLUSION

China's traditional environmental management efforts such as afforestation projects have both long-term environmental benefits and immediate economic value in timber production, agricultural windbreaks, watershed, and soil management. Nature preserves and the protection of rare and endangered species provide little in immediate productivity or even dependably predictable future economic benefits. Furthermore such projects are highly sensitive to changing governmental policy, political instability, agricultural shortfalls, and grass-roots nonchalance. Why, then, is China putting a well-publicized effort into protection of its rare and endangered species? The answer has not fully been stated, but some speculations are worth consideration.

One important motivation for the campaign is Chinese cultural pride and patriotism. Sources such as the *Beijing Review* mention international interest in rare and endangered Chinese species (e.g., April 5, 1982, p. 29). China has learned that the world scientific community favors the protection of endangered species. The Chinese also discovered that rare species hold great popular appeal in many countries. Perhaps it is even felt that the world sees effective management of endangered species as an indication of the effectiveness, virtue, and civilization of a nation and its government. At any rate, the Chinese have a sense that the world is watching to see how and with what sense of responsibility China manages these resources.

Certainly there is political value in China's unique possession of rare species such as the giant panda. What more elegant state gift can there be than a giant panda? What more appealing symbol of a friendly China than international cooperation in giant panda research?

The Chinese also see some economic potential in endangered species protection. In the short run, some wildlife may be adaptable to domestication or semi-domestication (much as native Alaskans are discovering present-day value in herding reindeer). Also, careful management of game animals is important because hunting is an important source of income to several hundred thousand Chinese annually (Greer and Doughty, 1976, p. 200). In the long run the gene pool potential may pay off. The economic value of nature preserves and protected wildlife to China's rapidly expanding tourist industry may also prove important.

Scientific and educational cooperation and exchanges involved with the preservation and study of endangered species have several values. For instance, a mutually satisfactory exchange may result if

Chinese scholars wish to study physics in the United States, but American scholars are more interested in Chinese wildlife than in Chinese physics. An additional rationale perhaps is that the Chinese feel that in their planned economy, all resources should be managed intelligently.

Whatever prompted the Chinese to support the protection of endangered species, they have decided to do so. The scale of their initial commitment is shown on the map supplement and demonstrates a significant beginning of a major environmental protection effort.

NOTE

1. I wish to thank the many scholars who assisted me with this research. Li Shumin of the Foreign Languages Group, Northwestern Polytechnic University, Xi'an, Shaanxi, PRC provided many hours of Chinese language tutoring and translation assistance. Chuan-Chu Chou of the Department of Biology, UCLA, was extremely generous in helping with translations and taxonomy. Dr. Stephen Anderson, Department of Biology, USC, helped with taxonomy as did Professor Charles Bennett and Professor Hartmut Walter of the Department of Geography, UCLA. Very special appreciation goes to the UCLA China Exchange Program and Zhongshan University, especially the geographers Professor Liang Pu, Professor Huang Jin, and Mr. Ji Hanyang. Mr. Ji did the handsome calligraphy in the table of protected wildlife on the back of the map supplement. UCLA provided several grants that helped me pursue this research and a grant for the printing of the map supplement. The Society of Woman Geographers also was most generous in providing a research grant that enabled me to go to China. Noel Diaz, cartographer at UCLA, was a frequent consultant while I drafted the map supplement. Professor Christopher L. Salter, UCLA, edited the manuscript and proofread the map supplement. Jim Nemeth also gave encouragement and assistance. Herbert Enderton and Bert Enderton provided editorial and computer assistance and endless support.

LITERATURE CITED

Allen, Glover M., 1938, *The Mammals of China and Mongolia.* New York: The American Museum of Natural History.

Beijing Review, 1981, (Nov. 23), p. 30.

_____ , 1982, (Jan. 25), p. 30.

_____ , 1982, (April 5), p. 28–29.

_____ , 1982, (Dec. 27), p. 13.

Boxer, Baruch and David Pramer, editors, 1978, *Environmental Protection in the People's Republic of China*. New Brunswick, New Jersey: Rutgers University Press.

CIA, 1979, *China, a topographic map at 1:10,000,000*. Washington, D.C.: CIA.

Cheng, Tso-Hsin, editor, 1964, *China's Economic Fauna: Birds*. Washington, D.C.: U.S. Department of Commerce, Office of Technical Services.

China Pictorial, 1982, No. 3.

China Reconstructs, 1982, (July), Beijing, pp. 10-13.

Clements, James F., 1978, *Birds of the World: A Check List*. New York: The Two Continents Publishing Group, Ltd.

Dili Zhishi (Geographical Knowledge), 1981, (July, No. 7), p. 12.

Dongwu Dili (Animal Geography), (full title: *Zhongguo Ziran Dili: Dongwu Dili*), 1979. Beijing: Ditu Chubanshe.

Greer, Charles E. and Robin Doughty, 1976, Wildlife utilization in China. *Environmental Conservation*, Vol. 3, No. 3, Autumn, pp. 200-208.

Lazell, James D., 1982, Are there lizards in this hotel? *Harvard Magazine*, Vol. 84, No. 5, 52-57.

Liu, Yukai, 1981, The present nature preserves in China and their distribution. *Ziran Ziyuan (Natural Resources)*, No. 2, 92-96.

Qu, Geping and Jinchan Li, 1981, Environmental management in China. *Unasylva*, Vol. 33, No. 134, 2-18.

Renmin ribao, 1980, (Oct. 22), p. 2.

Salter, Christopher L., 1973, *Doing Battle with Nature*. Eugene, Oregon: University of Oregon, Asian Studies Committee.

Schafer, Edward H., 1968, Hunting parks and animal enclosures in ancient China. *Journal of the Economic and Social History of the Orient*, Vol. 11, Part 3, October, 318-343.

Schaller, George B., 1981, Pandas in the wild. *National Geographic*, Vol. 160, No. 6, December, 735-749.

Schell, Orville, 1982, Journey to the Tibetan Plateau. *Natural History*, Vol. 91, No. 9, September, 48-57.

Shi, Guanfu, 1981, Our country's natural reserves. *Dongwuxue Zazhi (Chinese Journal of Zoology)*, No. 4, 41-45.

Sowerby, Arthur de Carle, 1914, *Fur and Feather in North China*. Tientsin.

Swannack-Nunn, Susan, Kenneth Bowman, and Patrick Heffernan, 1979, *Environmental Protection in the People's Republic of China*. New York: The National Council for U.S.-China Trade.

Thorhaug, Anitra, 1978, *Botany in China: Report of the Botanical Society of America*, Delegation to the People's Republic, May 20-June 18, 1978. Stanford: United States-China Relations Program, Stanford University.

Walker, Ernest P., 1964, *Mammals of the World*. Baltimore: The Johns Hopkins Press.

Ye, Rong, 1982, Bird Island on Qinghai Lake. *China Reconstructs*, July, p. 10.

Zhongua Renmin Gongheguo Dituji (National Atlas of the People's Republic of China), 1979. Beijing: Ditu Chubanshe.

Environmental Problems and the Development of Chinese Fisheries[1]

Jaydee R. Hanson

Despite expansion of the Chinese fleet and major advances in aquaculture, Chinese fishery yields in 1980 totaled approximately the same as those claimed by the Chinese 20 years earlier (Table 1). Per capita availability of fish in China during the late 1970s and during the 1980s amounted to less than 5 kilograms (kg) annually, a relatively low figure even for a developing country. Chinese planners have wanted to believe that they could optimize every aspect of development at once; only since 1977 have they freely acknowledged the major conflicts between fisheries development and other national goals. Numerous fishery officials and newspaper articles have charged that industrial pollution, land reclamation, and water projects severely limit the potential of fisheries throughout China. Production and distribution of fisheries products have been the prime goal of fisheries management since 1949. Conservation has received scant attention.

While all fisheries have suffered from environmental damage, freshwater-capture fisheries production (as opposed to aquaculture) declined the most. From the beginning of the 1960s China's output of naturally-grown freshwater fish fell annually, dropping from more than 600,000 metric tons to 300,000 metric tons by 1979 (Zhu, 1980). Other fisheries production did not decline that much, as the species composition of the catch changed from highly-valued food fishes to those of lesser worth.

142

WETLANDS RECLAMATION

Landscape modification is one of the most characteristic elements of China's agricultural transformation. In their desire to remake nature so that it will better serve agriculture, the Chinese frequently discounted alternative uses for the land. Wetlands, in particular, have been filled, with little regard for their alternative uses as floodwater catchments, fish and wildlife habitats, and spawning grounds and nurseries for many fish species. The filling of wetlands in localities with the most fertile fisheries caused fish catches to decline and reduced opportunities for development in the fishing industry. Cong Ziming, deputy director of the State Aquatic Products Bureau, in a *Guangming ribao* interview (Jia, 1979) attributed the shortages of freshwater fish in China's markets largely to massive reclamation of land surrounding freshwater lakes, ponds, and rivers for planting food crops. Cong accused the land reclaimers of having an incomplete understanding of slogans like "taking food production as the key link." These slogans and related campaigns, he feels, have led to the loss of more than 1.5 million ha of the most productive fisheries. Particularly hard hit are the six "water" provinces along the Changjiang (Yangtze), but every major fish-producing area has been affected. The shallowness of the Changjiang basin lakes makes them ideal for fish production, but the same shallowness makes the lakes easy to drain or fill. The very statistics that indicate success for an area's land-reclamation program may portend disaster for its fisheries.

Hubei, once known as "the province of a thousand lakes," has fewer than 500 lakes larger than 70 ha. Its total lake surface has been reduced by 75 percent to only 200,000 ha (Hu and Tian, 1981). Hunan's Dongting Hu now covers only 170,000 ha; its area decreased from 435,000 ha in 1949 (Liu, 1979; FBIS, March 20, 1979, L15). In Jiangxi 331 large dikes hold back the waters of Poyang Hu from 87,000 ha of reclaimed land. Only 26,000 ha of the lake remain in reserve for fishing. Eight carp nurseries within the lake have been destroyed, and 11 others have been seriously affected. Ten percent of the Tai Hu in Jiangsu have been converted to farmland (Jia, 1979).

During the Cultural Revolution some parties even encouraged the filling of fishponds as a way of achieving local self-sufficiency in grain production. Shanghai lost 5,500 ha of fishponds; Zhejiang lost 3,400 ha; and Guangdong lost 13,000 ha (Yang, 1978).

Sea fisheries likewise suffer from coastal reclamation efforts. Between 1959 and 1978 nearly 70,000 ha of fish- and shellfish-breeding grounds gave way to farm crops, resulting in the loss of tens of thousands of tons of marine products annually. Oyster, clam, and mullet production in Guangdong and Fujian suffered. Mussel production in Zhejiang dropped by 1,000 t annually as a result of grounds lost to landfill (Yang, 1978).

WATER CONSERVATION PROJECTS

China is justifiably proud of its achievements in building water conservancy projects. Over the past 30 years more than 80,000 reservoirs have been built (Anonymous, 1980a). Yet many dam, canal, and other water projects have not adequately cared for the needs of fisheries. Like the salmon of the U.S. Pacific Northwest, China's migratory fish are particularly affected by water projects which block their migration or greatly reduce water flow. The Reeve's shad (*Hilsa reevesi*) of the Changjiang, the freshwater crabs of Yangcheng Lake near Suzhou, and the crabs of Shengtang in Hebei were once among the most famous food fish in China; today the output of all three has shrunk drastically due to the blocking of waterways and insufficient water flow. Once the Tai Hu, Hong Ze Hu, Chao Hu, and Hong Hu teemed with black carp, grass carp, silver carp, and big head carp, but water conservancy projects blocked the outlets of these lakes resulting in the disappearance of highly valued carp (Yue, 1980).

Perhaps the best example of the failure to include fisheries' needs in overall planning is the nearly completed Gezhou Dam across the Changjiang. Despite injunctions from both Mao Zedong and Zhou Enlai to save the fish during the dam's construction, fish passages still have not been provided. Catches of carp, eel, and bream could be greatly reduced. The white sturgeon (*Huso dauricus*), the Chinese sturgeon (*Acipenser sinensis*), and the paddlefish (*Psephurus gladius*) may become extinct. Those opposed to providing fish the passages use three main arguments. First, the opponents argue that after the dam is built the fish will find new spawning grounds. Second, they believe that artificial breeding can restore populations.[2] Finally, the Chinese dam builders charge that fish structures would cost 20–30 million yuan which they believe cannot be justified. Chinese biologists and environmentalists, like their Western counterparts, argue that unique Chinese species, like the Chinese sturgeon and paddlefish, should be considered priceless national treasures and are certainly worth more for the production of roe alone than the 20 million yuan a fish passage would cost. Fish hatcheries and aquaculture, they argue, can supplement natural production, not replace it (Lu, 1980; Wang, 1981).

The potential for fish raising in reservoirs is likewise limited. Only two-thirds of China's 2 million ha of reservoir surface produce fish. The average yield of all reservoirs stocked with fish is only 85 kg/ha (Anonymous, 1980a). Even that figure is misleading because much of the total reservoir production comes from shallow reservoirs that are virtually fishponds. Here the potential would be much greater if more of the reservoirs had been cleared and graded so they could be more easily harvested. In Hubei province, despite the construction of several hundred reservoirs since the 1950s, fish catches of the 1970s average only about 22 percent of the 1950 averages (Lu, 1980).

INDUSTRIAL WASTES

China's factories daily dump more than 4,000 t of untreated industrial wastewater into its rivers, lakes, and seas. The waterways of China's industrialized Northeast are particularly polluted. All of Jilin Province's 140 rivers are fouled. The Songhua Jiang (Sungari) is now virtually devoid of fish (Yue, 1980). Some rivers are heavily polluted with heavy metals, and cases of mercury poisoning of people who have eaten fish have been reported (Pan, 1980).

Mining and oil production also contribute to aquatic pollution. From 70,000 to 80,000 t of crude oil have been discharged into the Yellow Sea and Bohai since 1974. This greatly affected the area's shrimp and scallop fisheries (Yue, 1980).

Fishermen in many areas have protested pollution of their fishing grounds, but action by factories and mines to reduce waste has been slow in coming (Anonymous, 1980b; Taihu Commune, 1980). Some factories even tried to assert that fish could grow anywhere, even in the wastewater from engines. The situation of fishermen near Changzhou, an industrial city in Jiangsu, seems to have become particularly critical. The fishermen of Wujin County fish in the Grand Canal and tributaries of the Beitang River. Until recently they caught 1,000 t of fish per year for sale in Changzhou. Now the grounds are polluted with phenol, kerosene, and other wastes from the Changzhou Refinery, the Changzhou Chemical Works, the Changzhou Chemical Dye Plant, the Changzhou Paper Mill, and the "East is Red" Printing and Dyeing Plant. Even when the fishermen catch fish, the fish cannot be sold because their phenol content exceeds health standards. In frustration over the loss of their livelihood, the Wujin fishermen marched on the factories in early 1980 to protest and to demand food. The industries were subsequently fined 50,000 yuan, but have reportedly not yet ceased pollution (Anonymous, 1980b).

Agricultural chemicals also reduce the yield from China's fisheries. During a visit to the Pearl River Freshwater Fisheries Institute outside Guangzhou in the summer of 1979, the author was told that the culture of fish in paddy fields is virtually impossible in many parts of South China due to increased usage of pesticides which harm both the fish and their prey. Moreover, in some areas organophosphate pesticides such as parathion and toxaphene are used as fish poisons, killing adult and juvenile fish (Zhang, 1980).

ENVIRONMENTAL PROBLEMS WITHIN THE FISHING INDUSTRY

By 1949, years of war resulting in the loss of many fishing vessels and much fishing effort had reduced China's catch to about 450,000 tons, less than one-third the pre-war peak in 1936 (Shindo, 1962). Vessel construction programs and expanded fishing after 1949 led to dramatic increases in fish catches. Within three years catches equaled the pre-war total. Catches in 1957 produced a record 3.116 million t, approximately seven times the 1949 total (Table 1). In 1958 scientists in Guangdong succeeded in their attempt to artificially spawn silver carp.

The dramatic increase in fish catches coupled with the potential for expanding aquaculture led many in the Chinese government to believe that all that was needed to increase fish production was to increase fishing effort; the resource, they believed, was limitless. This attitude, that fishery resources are limitless, fit well with the Great Leap Forward emphasis on sheer effort as a way of developing China. The official start of the "Great Leap" in fisheries came when the Minister of Aquatic Products announced that by 1962 China would be the biggest fishing power in the world (*Renmin ribao*, February 12, 1958).

By the spring of 1959 it was apparent that even more fisheries products would be needed to make up for shortages of other foods. All people's communes were urged to set up fishing units if possible (*Da Gong Bao*, May 10, 1958). In late March and early April the State Council lengthened the spring fishing season and issued a set of directives to encourage fisheries. Every effort was made to fish as long as possible and to catch as much as possible (*Renmin ribao*, April 14, 1959). The 1959 catch was reported as the largest China ever had. How much of this reported increase occurred is a matter of speculation but fishing effort on already stressed stocks increased.[3] Unfortunately, despite pleas for conservation by a few brave souls, Great Leap Forward programs in fisheries continued through 1960. No fisheries statistics were released between 1959 and 1977.

By 1961 the problems of the industry were openly discussed. For the first time both fisheries scientists and politicians recognized overfishing as a central problem of the fishing industry. In the seventh Plenum of the Western Pacific Regional Fisheries Research Commission, which met in 1962, Cheng Jufeng reported on the depletion of yellow croaker stocks.[4] He pointed out that irrational fishing of juvenile fish during the previous years led to the depletion of the resource (Cheng, 1964). Other reports in the press and scientific publications confirmed the decline in various other economic fish stocks. Nationwide fisheries regulations were promulgated in 1964. The regulations prohibited many of the most destructive fishing practices of the Great Leap Forward. By 1965 yields had nearly returned to 1957 levels (Table 1).

The Cultural Revolution (1966–1969) again caused a decline in fisheries production. This decline, however, can only in part be attributed to overfishing by the industry. Political activities, inadequate supplies, and unrepaired vessels forced many crews to remain in port during this period.

Fish production increased annually between 1970 and 1977. Yet this does not mean that the Chinese have solved their problems with overfishing. The Chinese were able to maintain their total production during the 1970s by shifting their efforts to less desired species as stocks of preferred species like croakers and herrings declined (Table 2). Many of the species which have not declined appreciably are being fished beyond their maximum sustainable yield (MSY), and the age composition of the catches is dropping. For example, Zhu (1980) calculated the MSY of Spanish mackerel fishery production in the Yellow Sea, East China Sea, and Bohai as 33,144 t (calculated with the Schaefer model) and as 35,125 t (calculated with the Fox model). This is very close to the actual catch in 1978 and higher than the 1979 estimates. Apart from filefish (*Cantherines* ssp.), the demersal species of both the East China Sea-Yellow Sea-Bohai region and the South China Sea region are fully exploited or overfished. Of all the major pelagic stocks, only chub mackerel

147

TABLE 1

Chinese Fisheries Production, 1949-1980[a]
(figures in thousands of metric tons)

Year	Production
1949	448
1950	912
1951	1,332
1952	1,729
1953	1,890
1954	2,293
1955	2,518
1956	2,648
1957	3,116
1958[b]	4,060
1959[b]	5,020
1965	2,984
1970	3,184
1971	3,495
1972	3,842
1973	3,931
1974	4,282
1975	4,412
1976	4,476
1977	4,695
1978	4,654
1979	4,305
1980	4,497

[a]includes dry weight of aquatic plants

[b]includes wet weight of aquatic plants.
Sources: For 1949-1958, State Statistical
Bureau, 1960; for 1959, *Renmin ribao*, 28 May
1960; for 1965, Jingji Dili Shiyensuo, 1980;
for 1970-78, Zhu, 1980; for 1979-80, *Beijing
Review*, 11 May 1981.

within the East China Sea is believed to have the potential to withstand the increased fishing effort (Zhu, 1980).

Perhaps the most disturbing trend in the development of China's marine fisheries is the increased reliance on shrimping as a major fishery. Heavy fishing for shrimp in the Bohai and Yellow Sea has already depleted many other larger fish species which do not reach sexual maturity as soon as do shrimp. Guo Renda estimates that during the major fishing seasons prime grounds, like those of the Bohai, are swept several times each day by the nets of some 10,000 vessels (Guo, 1980).

Such heavy fishing led to the ecological collapse of the Gulf of Thailand shrimp fishery. Even today in the Gulf of Thailand the fish of higher trophic levels have not returned. The starfish that replaced them have little economic value. Ironically, shrimp fisheries are one area in which China has turned abroad for development assistance. Nearly every major Chinese fishing corporation has signed contracts with Japanese or Hong Kong fishing concerns for help in modernizing their fleets. The Chinese receive refrigeration equipment, modern vessels, and other technology; the foreign company receives shrimp for a given number of years (Hanson, 1980).

Unfortunately, the foreign exchange benefits of making shrimp exports a center piece of Chinese fisheries development are obvious to planners;[5] the long-term environmental effects on other fisheries are apparently not so obvious. Unless some vessels are taken out of the fishery, the new vessels will simply increase the strain on a system that is already overfished both biologically and economically.

The marine culture of shellfish plays a major role in China's future development plans. Chinese officials hope that marine culture can provide jobs to unemployed fishermen and earn foreign exchange. During 1981 each coastal county of Guangdong was to develop and test a plan for transferring fishermen from fishing to marine-fish farming. Guangdong authorities hope that all surplus laborers in fishing units will transfer to fish-farming by 1985 (Fei, 1980). Even in this program adverse environmental effects are possible if counties reclaim mariculture coastal sites critical to the survival of marine species in the wild.

TABLE 2

Chinese Marine Catch: Yield of Major Species, 1970-1979[a]
(Figures in thousands of metric tons)

Year	Elongate Ilisha Herring	Large Yellow Croaker	Small Yellow Croaker	Filefish	Pacific Herring	Japanese Spanish Mackerel	Largehead Hairtail	Chub Mackerel	Fleshy Prawn	Paste Shrimp	Squid	Jelly Fish
1970	9.0	158.7	30.4	...	2.2	26.2	391.8	173.1	14.4	92.7	56.6	50.6
1971	12.4	143.8	34.0	...	30.9	...	429.6	36.6	13.2	77.1	73.3	16.1
1972	11.1	149.3	20.5	...	181.9	32.8	495.5	78.3	11.9	90.1	47.8	16.6
1973	...	137.9	31.9	...	120.5	36.5	564.5	93.1	32.6	...	...	58.2
1974	...	197.2	...	...	71.7	39.2	577.3	113.5	39.9	...	...	22.1
1975	...	140.0	...	...	57.6	33.5	483.8	84.5	29.1	...	...	17.1
1976	...	123.7	...	...	55.3	28.2	433.6	79.0	10.0	115.1	35.8	5.1
1977	...	91.2	...	230.1	17.5	38.2	392.5	134.9	25.1	171.9	40.4	11.7
1978	...	93.8	...	310.4	21.8	34.5	387.2	282.3	38.4	195.5	62.0	3.6
1979	14.7	82.9	35.6	105.4	38.9	30.0	437.2	250.0	33.0	98.1	42.4	12.9

[a]1970-1978 figures from Zhu, 1980. 1979 figures from FAO, 1980. 1979 catch data for Japanese Spanish mackerel, chub mackerel, and fleshy prawns are FAO estimates. (...) represents years for which no catch statistics were supplied.

RESOURCE MANAGEMENT AND ENVIRONMENTAL PROBLEMS IN CHINA'S FISHERIES

The preceding four sections described some of the kinds of environmental problems faced by the fishing industry in China. This section discusses some of the reasons these problems persist.

Many Western students of fishery resource problems believe that public ownership could avoid many of the problems of common property fisheries.[6] China's fisheries are publicly owned and yet they suffer from all the problems of open-access fisheries. The inability of the Chinese to adequately prevent externalities such as overfishing, water pollution, and land-use conflicts can be seen to have four major causes: 1) the failure to give fisheries significant attention in national economic planning; 2) the inadequacy of regulations governing the fishery; 3) the failure of pricing mechanisms to recognize the value of fisheries as opposed to other economic activities; and 4) the lack of effective administrative measures to implement the priorities of the plans and regulations.

FISHERIES AND NATIONAL PLANNING

Since 1949 the cabinet responsibility for fisheries has rested in no less than five different ministries or State Council agencies. China's Five Year Plans, provincial plans, and national campaigns over the last three decades, to be sure, included fisheries, but the slight attention given fisheries as an element in the economic system suggests that as an economic activity it was relatively insignificant.

While fisheries concerns were written into the plans, the lack of detail in the plans and the focus on production rather than on conservation created problems. Hydropower projects were not required by the plans to provide for fish migration. Industries and mines were not required to treat wastewater. Output was often the sole criterion for determining whether or not an industry met its plan. After all, what does cleaning water have to do with producing coal? When fisheries' needs conflicted with agricultural goals, the relative insignificance of fisheries in the state planning process became even clearer. At best, fisheries needs were not coordinated with those of grain production. Marshes were drained; shallow offshore areas were diked; and rivers were diverted in the massive campaigns to increase grain production. China's need for grain and the political values favoring self-reliance in grain production made producing grain the operational priority in the plans regardless of statements about the value of fisheries.

Inadequate information on the bio-economic aspects of fisheries contributed to the failure of planners to provide for fisheries. High production quotas assumed fisheries to be more productive than they in fact were and encouraged greater fishing effort than would have been desirable if more accurate data were available. Agricultural forecasting is difficult, but modeling a multi-species fishery, like that of the South China Sea, where one trawl can bring up to 40 different species, is next to impossible without the aid of a computer. Given the low priority of the fishing industry, it is not surprising that it was 1978 before Chinese fisheries scientists could use computers to help them model fisheries. More and better data on the biology and economics of their fisheries may help the Chinese to better integrate fisheries into their overall planning. Even in a socialist economy there are alternate uses for capital. Better data on the true cost and benefits of this undervalued resource can help managers choose between alternate uses of scarce capital.

FAILURE OF REGULATION

In 1957 the Ministry of Fisheries drafted regulations on the conservation of fishery resources. The start of the Great Leap Forward prevented the publicizing of the regulations. The State Council finally adopted the regulations in 1964 only to have them submerged in politics when the Cultural Revolution started. In March 1979 the national regulations were again made public (Zhu, 1980; FBIS, April 3, 1979, L16–19).

While Chapter 5 of the regulations for fisheries conservation includes provisions designed to protect fisheries from the negative consequences of pollution, water conservation projects, and land reclamation, the regulations must be considered inadequate in that they leave provincial authorities and state enterprises with the responsibility for "fine-tuning" and implementing the regulations. It might be argued that the more detailed planning and implementation of regulations should be the responsibility of lower levels of government; but, where there is significant migration of fish stocks across province borders, the regulations of any one province are likely to be inadequate. For example, if Fujian's croaker fishery is, in fact, based on the same stock as that of Guangdong, a lack of coordination between the two in the development of regulations could make regulations established by either meaningless. Fishing two-times the maximum sustainable yield of any stock is certainly overfishing. Likewise, many fishery problems of provinces along the Changjiang would be similarly interrelated.

152

More cooperation between provinces in the same region in fisheries' regulation and management could likely solve some of the problems. Yet regulations alone do not effectively integrate fisheries' concerns into the overall planning process. Enforcement of such regulations presents a problem. A regional fisheries unit involved in the planning of activities like dredging, irrigation facilities, pollution control, and land reclamation in the same area is likely to be ineffective.

The Chinese may also wish to adopt much more comprehensive regulations including not only seasonal and species limits, but also limits on where individual vessels can fish. Imports of new fishing technologies, however selective, will increase fishing efforts unless the existing fleet is limited. A licensing system, similar to that operating in Japan, where the near-shore waters are divided between different classes of vessels, could in effect allow for ownership of particular fishing grounds.

PRICING FAILURE

Chinese fisheries have suffered from two sorts of pricing failure: first, a failure to value the resource at all, and second, an undervaluing of the resource.

The failure to place a value, monetary or otherwise, on lakes, marshes, and seashores resulted in them being considered marginal. Thus, the opportunity costs have been perceived as supporting the conversion of these areas to 'productive' grain fields. Since these areas are owned by the state, labor is the only significant cost involved in their reclamation. Their roles as spawning areas for fish or as areas for related considerations seems to have been extraneous to the decision-making process. Or it was felt that substitutes could be found for such areas. An FAO delegation reports that the Chinese seem to "prefer to find alternative ways of fulfilling the ecological roles played by wetland and swamps (e.g., the anchored clumps of grass put out in the Tai Hu)" (Tapiador et al., 1977).

Another aspect of the price problem occurs when the prices do not reflect the true value of a resource. Marine fish, for example, are said to be priced too low to pay for the costs of their capture. State enterprises have received government subsidies independent of their profit or lack of profit. If wholesale prices are too low, small-scale fishermen may be encouraged to produce beyond their quotas as a means to receive additional income. These low prices moreover do not reflect the scarcity of the resource, and the low price for fish may discourage investments in the industry as a whole. A pricing structure which emphasizes weight alone, and not size, encourages fishermen to catch juvenile fish and stimulates overfishing. Were more data available, an analysis of the data would likely indicate severe economic overfishing as well as biological overfishing. China's fishery personnel are now being trained in how to better collect basic biological and economic data necessary for evaluating the health of fishery stocks. Until the Chinese industry integrates such analyses into its decision-making and price structure, production will remain the most important measure of fisheries management.

ADMINISTRATIVE PROBLEMS

Even if plans and regulations adequately address environmental problems, the problems will persist if the plans and regulations are ineffectively implemented or poorly enforced by administrators. China's fisheries regulations and plans have been violated in part, too, because the state itself has conflicting priorities. The 1979 fisheries regulations, like their 1964 counterparts, make provision for penalties for their violation, but the pattern of past violations suggests that the cost of complying with the regulations has been greater than noncompliance. If regulations are to be effective in reducing harmful fishing practices and in protecting the fishing environment, the state's administrators must convince individual factories, communes, mines, and other enterprises that their situation indeed will improve as a result of following the regulations. In any case, regulations must be enforced to be effective. During times of political turmoil in China regulations have simply been ignored. Even in a milder political climate regulations are unlikely to be fully enforced if the enforcing unit is the same as the producing unit. To the author's knowledge, even within the fishing industry there is no separate body charged with the specific task of enforcing conservation measures.

SUMMARY AND CONCLUSIONS

China's fishery development has suffered from many of the same sorts of environmental problems that plague fisheries development throughout much of the world. In China the destruction of fish

154

habitat through land reclamation and water conservancy projects seems to have especially affected freshwater-capture fisheries. Water pollution and overfishing have reduced catches of freshwater fish and the most preferred marine species. Total catch has grown, but only as there has been heavier fishing of less preferred species.

Since 1977 Chinese fisheries officials have given more and more attention to the environmental problems of the fishing industry. However, their environmental concern seems not to have been integrated into the planning of other sectors of the economy. New regulations alone will not solve the environmental problems of China's fisheries. To a large extent, whether or not these problems will be solved depends on the political will and priorities of the Chinese leadership. If the Chinese leadership decides to blindly focus on the economic benefits of modernization, the long-term viability of China's fisheries could be further undermined. Ui Jun, a Japanese environmentalist and the president of the Asian Environmental Society, believes that China's modernization plans could make China one of the pollution giants of the 21st century. He attributes much of China's pollution to administrative problems. The Chinese, he says, "haven't been able to solve the organization question. In pollution control, the Chinese must rely on the concern of the people at the top" (Ratner, 1981). For the sake of China's fisheries, it is to be hoped that Professor Ui's prediction will be proved wrong by a Chinese leadership which will be able both to develop China's natural resources and to protect the environment on which living resources depend.

NOTES

1. The author is grateful for discussions with staff members of the Zhujiang Freshwater Fisheries Research Institute in August of 1979 and members of the Chinese Aquaculture Delegation to the U.S. in October 1980. Their comments, while not directly incorporated into the text of this article, helped to clarify many issues raised in articles in magazines and newspapers.

2. Salmon hatcheries in the United States have restored the catch to a level above the low levels following the damming of rivers of the Pacific northwest, but catches in those rivers remain much lower than they were before the dams were built.

3. The Chinese apparently changed their statistical system for fisheries during the Great Leap Forward. Aquatic plants were included on a wet weight basis in the 1958 and 1959 figures. There is also the possibility that the 1958–59 figures were simply exaggerated.

4. The Western Pacific Fisheries Commission was established in 1956 as a joint fisheries research program of North Vietnam, North Korea, China, Mongolia, and the U.S.S.R. It is now defunct.

5. Fisheries exports in 1979 earned China $330 million, most of which came from shrimp sales, according to the State Aquatic Products Bureau (1980).

6. See, for example, Arlon Tussing's (1968) discussion of ocean fisheries in his *Alaska-Japan Economic Relations*.

LITERATURE CITED

Anonymous, 1980a, Water conservancy projects must better serve the overall development of fisheries. *Renmin ribao*, March 10, in Joint Publications Research Service (JPRS), No. 75502.

_____ , 1980b, Industrial waste water spells disaster for river fish. *Guangming ribao*, June 6, in JPRS No. 75927.

Beijing Review, 1981, (May 11).

Cheng, Jufeng, 1964, Xiao huangyu dili de yenjiu (Research on the distribution and abundance of the small yellow croaker). *Taiping Yang Xibu Yenjiu Weiyuanhui* (Proceedings of the Seventh Session of the Western Pacific Fisheries Research Commission). Beijing: Kexue Chubanshe, pp. 35-70.

Da Gong Bao, 1958, (May 10), cited in *China News Analysis*, No. 243, August 29, 1958, p. 3.

(FAO), Food and Agriculture Organization of the United Nations, 1980, *Yearbook of Fisheries Statistics, 1979*.

(FBIS) Foreign Broadcast Information Service, (references given only as dates and page numbers refer to *Foreign Broadcast Information Service: People's Republic of China*).

Fei, Hongnian, 1980, Utilization of ocean fishery resources urged. *Nanfang ribao*, August 7, in JPRS 76619.

Guo, Renda, 1980, Rational utilization of ocean fishery resources. *Haiyang Yuyue*, No. 5, in JPRS 78385.

Hanson, Jaydee, 1980, China's fisheries: scaling up production. *The China Business Review*, Vol. 7, No. 3, 25-30.

Hu, Leibin and Tian Zhuang, 1981, Water surfaces should be used in the same way as cultivated land. *Renmin ribao*, March 10, in JPRS 77878.

Jia Shumei, 1979, Interview with Cong Ziming, deputy director of the State Aquatic Products Bureau. *Guangming ribao*, January 11, in JPRS 72921.

Jingji Dili Shiyensuo (Economic Geography Research Lab), 1980 *Zhongguo Nongye Dili Zonglun (Atlas of Chinese Agricultural Geography)*. Beijing: Zhongguo Kexue Yuan (Chinese Academy of Sciences), pp. 309-327.

Liu, Guilian, 1979, Fish in Dongting lake need to be protected as speedily as possible. *Renmin ribao*, July 27, in JPRS 74551.

Lu, Xi, 1980, Don't forget about saving fish when building the Gezhou dam. *Guangming ribao*, June 27, in JPRS 76210.

Pan, Yunzhou, 1980, Mercury pollution in the Songhuajiang. *Huanjing Baohu* (Environmental Protection), No. 2, in JPRS 76753.

Ratner, Jonathan, 1981, An interview with environmental activist Ui Jun. *Environmental Action*, September, pp. 21-24.

Renmin ribao, 1958, (February 12), p. 10.

———, 1959, (April 14).

———, 1960, (May 28), p. 7.

Shindo, Shigeaki, 1962, *Sea Fisheries in Communist China*. Tokyo: Japanese Fisheries Resource Conservation Association.

State Aquatic Products Bureau, 1980, Protect aquatic resources and develop cultivation. *Gongren ribao*, April 8, in JPRS 76040.

State Statistical Bureau, 1960, *Ten Great Years*. Beijing: Foreign Languages Press.

Taihu Commune Revolutionary Committee, Shengsi County, Zhejiang, 1980, Letter to the editor: serious damage to the fisheries of our island by industrial waste water. *Guangming ribao*, October 22, in JPRS 77310.

Tapiador, D.D., H.F. Henderson, M.N. Delmendo, and H. Tsutsui, 1977, *Freshwater Fisheries and Aquaculture in China*. Rome: Food and Agriculture Organization of the United Nations.

Tussing, Arlon, 1968, *Alaska-Japan Economic Relations*. Fairbanks: Institute of Social, Economic and Government Research, University of Alaska.

Wang, Zhongren, 1981, Protection of Changjiang fish resources will brook no delay: an investigation of the problems of fish passages in the Gezhou Dam. *Renmin ribao*, February 18, in JPRS 77878.

Yang, Haiqun, 1978, Reclamation from the sea for building fields cannot displace sea breeding. *Renmin ribao*, October 18, p. 1, in JPRS 72921.

Yue, Ping, 1980, There should be a radical change in the guiding thought for fishery development. *Hongqi*, No. 23, December 1, pp. 16-20, in JPRS 77290.

Zhang, Zhonghuang, 1980, Stop excessive fishing, protect resources in the Zhujiang river system. *Nanfang ribao*, January 8, in JPRS 75682.

Zhu, Deshan, 1980, A brief introduction to the fisheries of China. *FAO Fisheries Circular*, No. 726.

Book Reviews

The Environment: Chinese and American Views. Laurence J.C. Ma and Allen G. Noble (eds.). New York: Methuen and Co., Ltd., 1981. 397 pages, illustrations, maps, index. $29.95.

Derived from a symposium held in late 1978, this edited collection presents perspectives on the environment by Chinese and American geographers. The volume, however, is more than a conference summary; it is a document signaling the resumption of professional contacts after decades of separation. With common intellectual roots, geography in the two countries is nonetheless quite different even, as this volume points out, when focusing on a common theme.

Utilizing the environment as a capacious umbrella capable of harboring disparate interests, the editors identify five broad topics to cluster the 24 chapters written by 28 authors: a) agricultural development, human settlement, and the environment; b) the impact of water on the environment; c) urban development and the environment; d) environmental monitoring; and e) environmental education and global problems. Although none of the parts fully examines each of these sub-themes, each part is preceded by a clearly written, but brief, introduction that places the following papers into a larger context.

The editors readily admit when a paper is an interim report or general survey. They include such papers with more analytical ones because the volume has less value in being comprehensive than in providing a broad reading of environmental concerns on both sides

158

of the Pacific. For the most part, the essays complement one another albeit without providing a rounded picture of each topic. In general, the Chinese essays portray a pragmatic sense of involvement with the earth. Wu Chuan-chun's contribution, for example, reiterates clearly and briefly the importance of agriculture to China and the unending transformation of the agricultural landscape. As an antidote to seeing increases in agricultural production as resulting only from myriad peasant efforts at the local level, the essay by Huang Ping-wei shows the utility of a macroscopic assessment of sunlight, temperature, and soil moisture as variables in guiding the pursuit of China's full agricultural potential. It is unfortunate that the survey by H.J. Walker on the human occupance of coastal areas makes so little reference to Chinese concerns with their littoral.

Four of the six chapters on water are by Chinese geographers, not an unexpected fact since hydrology and geomorphology are well developed strengths in Chinese geography. Except for the informative chapter on Chinese wetlands, these chapters emphasize fluvial processes and reveal an up-to-date awareness of English-language materials. Huang Hsi-chou's fine chapter on wetlands could have fitted well in the agricultural development section of the book since its concern is primarily with utilization possibilities.

Part III, emphasizing urban development and environment, is a potpourri of papers that range from one on water (suitable for the earlier section, as well) to useful papers on environmental perception and noise pollution, both fertile fields of interest to the Chinese. In another forum Professors Noble and Ma reveal the mingling of their research tasks with the Chinese context in a study of noise pollution in Chinese cities. Nothing exceptional is reported in Parts IV and V, focusing on environmental monitoring and environmental education; yet collectively the chapters force one to keep in mind the various scales that must be confronted in assessing accurately and utilizing effectively the environment.

It is unfortunate that some of the Chinese concerns regarding environmental problems are not addressed. Without drawing attention to the reality of air and water pollution in China, it is only too easy to perceive Chinese efforts as wholly successful. In the several years since the Sino-American symposium which fathered this volume, Chinese authorities candidly have expressed their concern for the environmental degradation that has accompanied industrial and agricultural development in China. The adoption in late 1979 of an Environmental Protection Law and its subsequent enforcement have had some impact on abating pollution and heightening the awareness of responsible persons. Those interested in the context of Chinese environmental views may wish to consult the chapters by Baruch Boxer ("Environmental Science") and Clifton W. Pannell ("Geography") in *Science in Contemporary China*, edited by Leo Orleans (1981) and reviewed in this issue.

The volume does contain information that is new and useful but also a good deal that is repetitious survey. Specialists in this country are likely to encounter little in these chapters by the American contributors that they haven't seen elsewhere; indeed, the Americans all have published widely in their field. What they will learn from the Chinese contributors is more in a comparative context than in methodological innovation. The Chinese geographers seem well aware of research efforts in the West. The editors would have increased the value of the book if they had included summaries of the discussions which must have accompanied the oral presentations at Wingspread. Deriving much of its value as a chronicle of the reestablishment of professional contacts, the volume reveals parts of the range of environmental interests of geographers. Stimulated in part by the personal relationships nurtured by reciprocal visits, it seems likely that some trans-Pacific scholarly collaboration may develop. Allen G. Noble and Laurence J.C. Ma should be commended for conceiving and nourishing these relationships.

–Ronald G. Knapp
SUNY New Paltz

South China in the Twelfth Century, A Translation of Lu Yu's Travel Diaries, July 3–December 6, 1170. Translated and edited by Chun-shu Chang and Joan Smythe. Hong Kong: Chinese University Press, 1981, Distributed by the University of Washington Press, Seattle. 250 pages, illustrations, map, notes, indexes, bibliography. $18.50.

In the 12th century, "South China" still included the Yangtze Valley country, and this travel account refers to the Yangtze River. The zone of territory covered comprised the shores of the southernmost section of the Grand Canal and the Yangtze River west of the canal crossing to a point in the western section of the Yangtze Gorges. Those areas included spots accessible on walks from mooring stops along the route. The author was a mid-level government civil official traveling from his home in Shang-yin (modern Shao-hsing, Shaoxing), Chekiang (Zhejiang) to K'uei-chou (Feng-chieh, Fengjie), in eastern Szechwan (Sichuan), to a new posting as Prefectural Vice-Administrator of K'uei-chou Province. K'uei-chou city on the Yangtze River, during the Sung period, was the chief administrative center of a region that included most of modern Kweichow (Guizhou) Province and much of what now is eastern Szechwan.

Lu Yu was a well educated member of a distinguished scholar-official family, but he never achieved appointment to any very high post. So, he occupied himself in writing. The journey recorded here was a long one by boat, some 1,800 miles, completed in 157 days, but actual travel movement occurred in only 77 days or parts thereof. The balance of the time was spent visiting with officials at government centers along the way, in taking short side trips to notable locations, or in waiting out bad weather or water conditions.

The volume does not comprise a systematic geographical commentary on conditions along the route, though his descriptions of the Yangtze Gorges are more explicit than those elsewhere. To employ a contemporary label, the diary provides an articulate "perception" study of some scenic landscapes, historic places, temples, and public building architecture, and literary comments by numerous famous poets. T'ang Dynasty poets Li Po and Tu Fu, and Sung Dynasty poet Su Tung-p'o are among those most frequently quoted as the author reacted to particular views of landscapes, scenes, and buildings. The diary might, therefore, be classified as geography via literature. The author had a strong historical consciousness, an acute sense of genealogy, and emphatic literary and artistic tastes. Only occasionally did he engage in mundane commentary on local conditions and the affairs of the plebeian folk who were officialdom's justification for existence. Sometimes he noted that improvements had been made in temples and public buildings since he had last visited the sites, but more often he commented that such no longer were the magnificent structures that authors of earlier centuries had described. Many old ruins, along with existing structures, he accounted for by naming the sponsors who had them built, and in what period.

The author's historical awareness comes out in comments relating happenings at a given place, and in noting name changes for settlements and buildings. The sense of genealogy shows up in the recording of personal, family, and dynastic relationships of former notables and the officials and monks with whom the author visited, dined, drank (water, tea, and wine), and viewed the various notable

161

sights. Lu apparently had previously written a classification of the qualities of water from wells, springs, and streams, water to drink straight (unboiled) and with which to make tea, and there are frequent comments on this subject.

The diary of the trip usually has been printed as a single unit in Lu's collected writings. Those writings have been reprinted many times, either separately or in collectanea. The first reprint was produced in the 13th century; the last edition was published in 1977. The present volume is the only translation of the diary into English that has been published. Joan Smythe had a translation in preliminary form at her death, and a mostly new translation and editing are the efforts of Chun-shu Chang. The latter translator-editor also has an acute sense of history and genealogy. Since Lu occasionally misquoted or made only cryptic comment on things or people, a large amount of editorial comment was felt necessary. In mechanics, therefore, the diary itself occupies only about 75 pages of this 250-page book, the rest being taken up in explanatory notes, bibliographic reference, and general editorial comment.

There are interesting tidbits of comparative nature throughout the volume. On a hot night (in late July) at a dinner in Chen-chiang (Chin-kiang, Zhenjiang) where the itinerary shifted to the lower Yangtze River, Lu noted that the plates of ice placed around the dining room had no effect at all, and that the tea served was very bad. A few nights later, at a mooring on the Yangtze River, mosquitoes were so bad that the travelers rigged their mosquito nets, but this was the only mention of that problem. Where the clear waters of Ku-shu Creek entered the Yangtze, at T'ai-ping chou (near modern Ma'anshan, upstream from modern Nanking, Nanjing), fish were so plentiful and cheap that "Day after day even our servants ate them to repletion." At a dinner in a pavilion on the city wall, in bright moonlight, the shadows were reflected in Ku-shu Creek such that Lu remarked "For the first time I realized how wonderful is the line by (Su) Tung-p'o, 'A jade pagoda rests in the gentle waves.'" Later on, as Lu's boat reached the entrance to P'eng-li Lake (Poyang Lake), he commented, "In all directions the view was limitless. Then I realized the beauty of Li Po's line, 'Setting sail, we entered a mirror of sky.'" Such perceptive reactions occur throughout the diary.

Lu spent a week at O-chou (Wuchang, of the Wuhan urban complex), was impressed by the number of boats on the river, enjoyed several dinners and the most notable local sights, and made a visit to Han-yang (Hanyang, the modern industrial unit of the Wuhan complex), but made no mention of Hankow (the chief

162

commercial unit of the Wuhan complex before 1949), though it was already a long-settled and famous site. West of O-chou, the travel route led off the Yangtze River into the inland water cutoff, the Chuan Ho (Pien Ho), which was traveled to Sha-shih (Shasi, Shashi). Villages along the Chuan Ho were rare and small, and there were reported many wolves and tigers. During the summers the region was largely a watery wasteland of rushes and tall grass, the channel was not navigable during winter low water, and there was much burning of the grasses at that period. At Sha-shih Lu's party shifted to a craft built to navigate the Yangtze Gorges, took on sculls and more crew, along with bamboo cable for tracking over the rapids to be encountered later.

This is not a volume for everyone interested in China, unless by chance there is an interest in the historical genealogy of places, temples, and relationships between classes of officialdom. It does provide some historical comparison between pre-T'ang and T'ang dynasty governmental spatial management systems with those of the Sung Dynasty. It is, however, an interesting account of travel and the ways of officialdom during the late 11th century, when the world moved at a pace different from that of today, and it is a good documentation of the behavioral tendencies of one middling Chinese bureaucrat.

–J.E. Spencer
University of California, Los Angeles

China's Island Frontier: Studies in the Historical Geography of Taiwan. Ronald G. Knapp (ed.). Honolulu: University Press of Hawaii, 1980. 196 pages, illustrations, maps, tables, graphs, indices, glossary of terms. $20.00 (hardcover).

Studies by eight geographers, two historians, and an anthropologist have been combined in a package dealing with the historical geography of Taiwan. Every chapter has a core of historical material, and several chapters review their subjects by periods of rule by the Dutch, the Ch'eng (Koxinga) family, the Ch'ing (Manchu) dynasty, the Japanese, and the Nationalists. Only two chapters do not open with something about the 17th century beginnings of the Chinese on the island. Nominally divided into two sections, six chapters fall under the heading, "Migration and Rural Settlement," and five fall under the title, "Urbanization and

163

Economic Integration," but there is not that much difference in relative concerns. Numerous maps, charts, tables, and a few photos assist the subject matter, and there are copious notes on bibliographic sources, plus a glossary of Chinese terms.

The first unit opens with a Chinese historian mining the sources on the beginnings of Chinese settlement prior to 1683, and focusing on the 17th century roles of the Dutch and the Ch'eng family. In the second paper, an historical geographer discusses the non-Chinese native inhabitants; the writer is concerned only with how Chinese settlement affected the changing locational distribution of the non-Chinese as occupation of the island progressed. The classical patterns show up: infiltration, land takeover, enforced taxation, pacification campaigns, native uprisings, highland reservations, and resettlement programs. A geographer reviews early Chinese settlement in the T'ao-yuan area of northwest Taiwan, dispells some classic notions about Chinese settlement habits, and interprets the pattern of rural settlement as dependent upon land tenure systems. A study by an historian of frontier settlement in the northeast, the I-lan basin, brings out the opportunistic role of the frontier entrepreneur, unrestricted by government but unassisted by large-scale backing or military colonization. Another historian's study of social violence focuses on the roles of voluntary associations during the Ch'ing period. Sworn brotherhoods, secret societies, religious organizations, plus mutual antipathy between groups coming from different mainland home regions, and a shortage of women and normal family structures were all elements in a complex social structure. On a frontier faced with the minimal presence of government, these features made for an unusually large number of peasant revolts and cases of communal strife. A geographer closes out the first unit with a study of Taiwanese place-names ranging from aboriginal to post-Japanese, in which the sequent occupance theme reveals types of names from every historical period, and some points of difference show up between mainland and island systems.

The second division opens with a geographer's historical survey of the growth and development of the walled city on Taiwan. Most city walls began as thorny bamboo palisades, advanced to earthen construction, and terminated in stone-brick facing over the earthen walls. The 17 Taiwan city walls enclosed comparatively small areas. The anthropologist among the authors contributed an economic history of the now small town of Lu-kang on the middle west coast. Originally a minor river-mouth "port," Lu-kang's "port," through the vagaries of coastal sedimentation, was temporarily free of silt in the mid-18th century. For a century, roughly 1760–1860, the "port" of Lu-kang was the leading exporter of rice to the mainland. Silting brought its decline, though its internal trade system continued. Three geographers combine a statistical study of nodal accessibility and connectivity for both highways and rail lines. The indices for highways indicate a progressive shift northward for both, and those for railways indicate a shift southward for both. A geographer contributes a study of the pushcar rail network that evolved on the T'ao-yuan plain in the northwest after 1895, under the Japanese, and continued until the late 1930s. Light narrow gauge rails permitted small platforms on wheels, termed *daisha*, pushed by one or two men each, to carry passengers or freight. At its peak in the 1920s, more than 800,000 tons of cargo and more than 5,000,000 passengers per year were being moved on just less than 1,400 kilometers of tracks. The final chapter is a geographer's historical economic study of the cane planting and sugar refining industry on Taiwan. Cane was present when Chinese settlement began, and its commercial importance expanded as the Dutch East India Company shipped sugar to Japan. Sugar exports have been a major foreign exchange earner in the past, but increasing home consumption and the vagaries of the world sugar trade may spell the decline of earnings in the future.

Owing to the presence of author interests, there are some peculiarities in the volume. The reader learns of the locations and of the moves of many of the 23 groups of pre-Chinese inhabitants, but the reader learns nothing of the cultural relations of these groups. The anthropologist does write good economic history. The transport networks study claims coverage from 1600 but, obviously, can employ statistically manipulable data only. One casual page is devoted to the numerous early coast-inland transport-trade networks, which focused on the west coast "ports" and which made possible, for example, the rise of Lu-kang as the premier rice exporter. This leaves untouched a whole sector of historical economic geography. The eastern coastal zone gets short shrift in this volume, and one would have liked a paper on some east coast theme. This is a volume that will be very useful to those interested in Taiwan, since it does present very soundly such a wide range of subject matter.

–J.E. Spencer
University of California, Los Angeles

China, A Geographical Survey. T.R. Tregear. New York: Halstead Press, John Wiley & Sons, 1980. 372 pages, illustrations, maps, tables, bibliography, index. $34.95 (hardcover).

There are a number of perspectives a reviewer can take on any book. Two of the most important ones for a college textbook are the book's accuracy and utility in the classroom. Professor Tregear's most recent volume on the People's Republic of China is particularly responsive to such a tandem review because of the very few comparative titles currently in print, and because of the role that he has played in the past two decades with his China geographies.

In *China, A Geographical Survey* (1980), T.R. Tregear has authored the third in his textbook trilogy on China, following his 1965 *A Geography of China* (Aldine) and his 1970 *An Economic Geography of China* (American Elsevier). The 1980 Halstead-Wiley volume is actually heavily indebted to the two earlier works. Cartography, tables, and much of the assessment of China's progress were initially developed in the 1965 volume and have been carried forth in significant measure. In a sense, this is as it should be, for China's historical depth makes it unlikely that patterns of geographic and even economic development which are thousands of years old will diverge dramatically in less than a generation. One might even find occasion to ask why an update of George Cressey's 1934 *China's Geographic Foundations* is necessary, or why J.E. Spencer's *Asia, East by South* (1954) and its generous China section needs to be augmented. But we know the answer to these shallow questions...even in China things do change and change rapidly. And, increasingly, outsiders have been able to gather information that provides the basic elements of such change. A current book, therefore, should give some energy to charting the development that has taken place since earlier major books, especially if such initial volumes are by the same author. On this front, Tregear's 1980 text is frustrating.

In the Select Bibliography in the 1980 volume, for example, it is bothersome to note that of the 260 sources—each quite varied and drawing from standard volumes, JPRS translations, English-language journals, and Chinese materials in translation—we find that only eight sources are from 1970 or later. That means that the great bulk of the material of the current volume was already dealt with in the 1970 economic geography, and a considerable portion had already played a major role in the writing of the 1965 book. All of us know the endless flow of material that comes into our offices or at least into our campus libraries and what a chore it is to attempt to stay current. Even the most diligent scholars fall behind now and again. But to produce a major text on China after the overthrow of the Gang of Four and have most of the source material for the book predate the beginning of the Cultural Revolution is to miss an important opportunity for useful analysis. Lines such as "The advocacy of late marriage and smaller families has been vigorously preached throughout the country. A three-child family is regarded as the ideal" (p. 213) to be published in 1980 misrepresent the speed and force with which the Chinese government upgraded its governmental exhortation of one-child families by as early as 1978. Inaccuracies such as this diminish the text's usefulness as a reference work and, unfortunately, set seeds of doubt about the overall currentness of the volume in the mind of the reader.

Currentness, however, must not be the only criterion by which a book is judged. A geographic textbook must have clarity in its goals, balance in its presentation of sometimes contested data, thoroughness in its discussion of key factors in the shaping of a place, and directness in the enumeration of essential facts. On these fronts, *A Geographical Survey* does a creditable job. Tregear has organized the book around traditional regional guidelines with two-thirds of the book focused upon themes of a developmental and systematic nature. Physical and historical geography are given concise but useful treatment as in Tregear's earlier two books. Discussion of development is centered upon the agricultural sector with chapters on contemporary agricultural development, agricultural production, and agricultural regions. Chapters that are too brief deal with communication, transport, population, and power, lulling the reader into a deceptively comfortable sensation of these phenomena being well under control. Industrial development and foreign trade are discussed in the two final chapters before the remainder of the book is given over to geographical regions. A short essay, "The Unity of China," seems almost a lift from the 1965 *China*, but, again, elements of unity in China do have a timelessness that makes such reiteration less of a redundancy than it might appear in other literature.

What Tregear has authored, then, is a third edition of an orthodox geographical study of China. As it stands, it is more complete and better illustrated than any other geography of China in print, and, as such, it serves the profession reasonably. Had a reader not seen the 1965 and 1970 texts, this 1980 tome could be read and welcomed as a tidy study on the diverse and regionally distinct peoples and places of the People's Republic of China. Even in concert with the earlier works, this book stands up as a basic text that can support a class with some success if it is appropriately used in teaching the geography of China.

This leads me to the second part of this review.

At the outset, I pointed out that a textbook should be evaluated for its utility in the classroom as well as its scholarship. Tregear's most recent book is a good support book for a regional class. The short and compact studies it offers on a wide variety of geographic elements in China allow a class to cover many themes while affording a professor an opportunity to elaborate on the specific ones in which he or she is most interested. The chapter on physical geography, for example, lends itself to elaboration on a number of themes. The topographic outlines given by Tregear may be compared with Spencer's provocative checkerboard pattern outlines in the 1954 edition of *Asia, East by South* while detailed discussion of the cultural role of these physically distinct areas can be well developed through lecture and slides. See if the class catches the caption switch on p. 14 and use that pair of graphics to highlight the tremendous variation in relief realized in China. Have the class articulate regional images of the areas chronicled under climatic regions (pp. 24–28) and then see how these compare with later representations gleaned from the final third of the book.

Historical geography affords the same sort of base for personal expansion and class research. Tregear touches on enough major elements in the historical development of China that many of your students, who often come from the history major, can take themes such as Yang Shao and Long Shan, the Great Wall, Chinese southward expansion, and water conservancy, and expand upon Tregear's geographic context in their own research. The base that the text establishes is adequate for a non-geographer to begin to understand the nature and significance of the geographic perspective, but there is much left to be added by additional reading or lecture. Tregear's use of Ssu-ma Ch'ien is a particularly rich addition and provides a grand intersection between historical chronicles and the geographic concern with landscape management and manipulation.

An additional utility that the book has for a class on the regional geography of China is illustrated in the discussions of agriculture. Tregear gives considerable space to the discussion of the Eight-Point Agricultural Charter of 1958 (pp. 111–128), and this section serves as a good base for instruction regarding the Chinese efforts to modify their agricultural patterns within traditional skill and technology. Any one of these eight programs can serve as a foundation for considerably expanded detail in discussion of current

168

as well as traditional solutions to the problem of food and fiber in China. To be able to work with mainstream governmental policy guidelines gives a class a good sense of involvement with contemporary decision-making and, in some cases, policy implementation. Tregear utilizes such campaigns widely, although he does so less than does Keith Buchanan in his 1970 *Transformation of the Chinese Earth.*

Finally, the regional section of *China, A Geographical Survey* serves as a good framework for an approach that many geographers continue to prefer in the teaching of a regional course. In Tregear's treatment the final third of the book provides both an introduction of some new material at a finer scale than that in the broad systematic chapters of the first two-thirds of the volume. There is also some reintroduction of earlier material so that the student gains an opportunity for some review as the regional map is fleshed out in prose, map, and table. The treatment includes short chapters on Taiwan and Hong Kong.

In conclusion, this text is a book that is likely to be faulted for its failure to have brought the most current information to press, or because of its sometimes bland treatment of governmental statistics. Beyond such shortcomings, however, the book should be noted for broad coverage, reasonable cartographic treatment of diverse information, a rich collection of Chinese government photographs, an interesting utilization of literary and historical sources, and some very useful tables. While the volume probably will not have the staying power of the earliest works of Cressey and Spencer, it does make a useful choice for the current study of the geography of modern China. Let the ambitious professors augment it with more contemporary readings and let the more part-time China geographers work to have classes understand the substantial material that is there. The book will serve both situations well.

–Christopher L. Salter
University of California, Los, Angeles

Science in Contemporary China. Edited by Leo A. Orleans, with the assistance of Caroline Davidson. Stanford: Stanford University Press, 1980. 599 pages, illustrations, maps, tables, appendices, index of personal names and institutions. $35.00 (hardcover).

The contemporary China field has a curious pioneer nature about it. The literature of both China geography and China analysis in general contains a steady stream of publications that derive from "short visits to China and an intense few days in meetings." Such reportage is traditionally associated with new exploration in a heretofore unknown region. Is China such a region? The answer we are inclined to give, with some ambivalence, is that much of China is new to the outside world. Or, more exactly, much of what we are seeing now reflects considerable effort on the part of the Chinese to transform tradition, and such campaigns warrant careful analysis by sinologists everywhere. Such fascination with the Chinese exploration of new organizational structures causes considerable ink to be given to premature and superficial evaluations.

I open this review with that observation because this volume—*Science in Contemporary China*—presents sinologists with a masterful example of what detailed analysis can be extracted from personal encounter and bibliographic diligence in the China field. In a time of frequent speculation concerning the direction in which China is heading, the scientists whom Leo Orleans (and Walter Rosenblith) brought together for this collaborative effort evince firm belief in the PRC's dedication to steady and continuing progress in scientific education and research.

A sense of the certainty with which the writers have authored their papers is given by Jack Harlan in the opening to his study on plant breeding. "Regardless of ideology, genetics is genetics and plant breeding is plant breeding...it is impossible to repeal fundamental laws of biology." He goes on, however, to acknowledge that "plant breeding and genetics in the PRC have uniquely Chinese characteristics" (p. 295). The volume is a careful study of the state of science in China, but within the context of the special circumstances that make China so interesting.

The scope and substance of the volume are shown in this list of titles and authors: "Science in China's Past"—Nathan Sivin; "Science Policy and Organization"—Richard P. Suttmeier; "Pure and Applied Mathematics"—Saunders Mac Lane; "Physics"—Nicolaas Bloembergen; "A Technical Note on High Energy Physics"—L.C.L. Yuan; "Chemistry"—John D. Baldeschwieler; "Astronomy"—Leo Goldberg; "Geography"—Clifton W. Pannell; "Earth Sciences"— Edward C.T. Chao; "Meteorology"—Richard J. Reed; "Fisheries, Aquaculture, and Oceanography" (edited by Caroline Davidson); "Basic Biomedical Research"—H.M. Temin; "Biomedical Research: Clinical and Public Health Aspects"—Myron E. Wegman; "Plant Breeding and Genetics"—Jack R. Harlan; "Plant Protection"—Robert L. Metcalf and Arthur Kelman; "Animal Sciences"—Thomas B. Wiens; "A Note on Agricultural Mechanization"—Leo A. Orleans; "Engineering"—Chang-Lin Tien; "Energy"—Vaclav Smil; "Electronics"—Bohdan O. Szuprowicz; and "Environmental Science"— Baruch Boxer. There is a concluding section on social sciences with an introduction and an essay by Harry Harding and short pieces by Jerry Norman, Kwang-chih Chang, Albert Feuerwerker, Dwight H. Perkins, and Jerome Alan Cohen. The introductory essay for the volume is by the editor, Leo A. Orleans.

While each China geographer can find a number of chapters that will serve his or her interests, the chapters by geographers Clifton W. Pannell, Baruch Boxer, and Vaclav Smil are the ones that speak most directly to China geography. Pannell's piece derives in part from discussion and conversations in which he was involved during the July–August 1977 delegation of American geographers invited to the PRC by the Chinese Academy of Sciences. His references present an extensive itemization of sources on geography in China. Boxer's discussion of environmental policies comes from Chinese materials in translation, (FBIS and JPRS), a number of Chinese journals, and several Western studies on environmental protection in the PRC. Vaclav Smil draws from a corpus of work similar to that of Professor Boxer's, but Smil adds a number of items from Russian and Western energy literature.

These three articles present an interesting range of approaches to evaluation of aspects of science in China, and some elaboration may serve to illustrate the variety that exists in this volume. Both Pannell and Smil tend to marshal considerable factual material to develop a highly detailed image of not only the actual state of geography and energy development in China today, but also to show the use of science in the organization of resources in the service of those two fields. Pannell talks of some of the technical aids utilized in cartography, geomorphology, hydrology, and remote sensing. The real service of science, however, in the field of geography seems to be focused on Chinese attempts to achieve a rational regionalization of resources. Such a patterning of economic development and urban growth within such systems of planning and construction appears to be a, if not the, significant goal for the utilization of geography in China's promotion of the Four Modernizations. The active work in geomorphology and hydrology does not seem to support the national goal of science working for the nation, but rather represents scientists making determined efforts to stay current with international standards of procedure and rigor.

It is economic geography that draws major attention in the articles of all three geographers. Boxer points out that China continues to suffer from the classic priority given to productivity as he notes "...production has always had the highest priority, [thus] protection needs have suffered, and there are few incentives for industrial ministries to invest funds in pollution control" (p. 466). Smil chronicles this Chinese interest in expanding economic growth when he says that "...accelerated development of energy resources was placed second (after agriculture) among the eight spheres singled out for special attention in the eight-year plan (1978–85) for scientific modernization" (p. 407). Smil gives considerable space to presentation of the nature of the technological level that China has attained in energy extraction from the resources that the nation possesses.

Pannell and Smil see China as being caught in a technology lag of approximately 15–20 years. Boxer chronicles the same general sort of time frame and gives detailed discussion of the particularly effective and modern efforts being made in China's Northeast in environmental management and the "integrated development of pollution control and material-recycling facilities in a complex of extractive and fabrication industries" (p. 471). A pattern, then, emerges of China being highly interested in gaining access to the state-of-the-art scientific methods in energy extraction and environmental management. But such techniques must put economic production and development first and foremost.

For the interested China geographer, as Boxer points out, material of value may be gleaned from numerous papers in this rich and detailed collection of windows on current Chinese scientific research activities and supporting facilities. Whether reading in the works done by the geographers or the dozen and a half other contributors, one gains a sense of chapter and verse of how the Chinese are utilizing science to move the nation toward more rapid scientific and economic development. While much writing on China may have the ring of explorers returned from short junkets, this volume reads like it was written by patient insiders blessed with keen observational skills and supported by good libraries. This is a very valuable collection.

–Christopher L. Salter
University of California, Los Angeles